· Books by Helene Hanff ·

Underfoot in Show Business
84, Charing Cross Road
The Duchess of Bloomsbury Street
Apple of My Eye

Underfoot in Show Business

· HELENE HANFF ·

Underfoot in Show Business

Little, Brown and Company · Boston · Toronto

Underfoot in Show Business was originally published by Harper & Row in 1962. It
has been revised for this edition.

LIBRARY OF CONGRESS CATALOGING IN PUBLICATION DATA
Hanff, Helene.
  Underfoot in show business.

  1. Hanff, Helene—Biography. 2. Authors,
American—20th century—Biography. 3. Stuart, Maxine.
4. Theater—New York (City) I. Title.
PS3515.A4853U5 1980   818'.5403 [B]   80-14788
ISBN 0-316-34319-6

BP
Designed by Susan Windheim

PRINTED IN THE UNITED STATES OF AMERICA

· *To the Reader* ·

You may have noticed this book was not written by Noel Coward. It's a book about show business, where fame is the stock in trade, and it's written by a name you've never heard of and probably can't pronounce. There is a simple explanation for this.

Each year, hundreds of stagestruck kids arrive in New York determined to crash the theatre, firmly convinced they're destined to be famous Broadway stars or playwrights. One in a thousand turns out to be Noel Coward.

This book is about life among the other 999. By one of them.

HELENE HANFF

Underfoot
in Show Business

·1·

Flanagan's Law

WE'LL BEGIN WITH THE LAW that governs the life of every one of the 999 from the day he or she first arrives in New York, which was first explained to me by a stage manager named Bill Flanagan. Flanagan's law of the theatre is:

No matter what happens to you, it's unexpected.

You can even work it backward. Thus if you know I never got anywhere in the theatre you can deduce from Flanagan's Law that my theatrical career must have got off to a magnificent start. And it did, back home in Philadelphia on the shining day when I got a letter from Theresa Helburn, co-producer of the Theatre Guild.

This was at the tag end of the Depression, and after one year of college I'd had to quit and go to work. I got a job as typist in the basement of a diesel-engine school. Twelve dollars a week and all the grease I could carry home on me. In my spare time I wrote plays. And one evening when I came home from work, my mother told me she'd heard on the radio that an organization called the Bureau of New Plays was sponsoring a playwriting contest. It was open to "young people of college age" and the three winners were to be awarded $1,500 fellowships.

"I sent away for an application blank for you," she said.

The application blank arrived and informed me I could submit as many plays as I chose. I'd already written three, but reading them over I didn't like any of them much. It was only October and since the deadline for submissions was January 1, I decided to write some new ones for the contest.

In the next three weeks, during lulls in the diesel-engine basement and at home in the evening, I wrote a new three-act play, since writing a three-act play takes no time at all when you haven't got any idea what you're doing. At the end of the three weeks I was fired, leaving me free to write three more plays during November and December. I sent all four off to the contest. And then, since the results weren't to be announced till March 15, I put the whole thing out of my mind and went job-hunting.

I landed a nice quiet situation as secretary to two musicians — a band leader and a saxophone player-teacher — who shared an office. The dance band played mostly subdebutante parties. In order to sell his band to the subdebs' mothers Van, the band leader, had to know well in advance when the approved boys' schools had their Christmas and Easter vacations, since no mother scheduled a party without assuring her daughter a good long "stag line." So part of my job was to write haughtily condescending letters to the headmasters of Andover, Exeter, Hotchkiss, Lawrenceville and so forth, requesting the dates of their holidays "in order to facilitate the planning of the coming social season." I signed the letters *Baroness Helena von Hanff, Social Secretary.*

My two bosses played in a luncheon-music ensemble in the Ritz-Carlton dining room so they were entitled to a Ritz mailbox and enough Ritz stationery for me to write the letters on. After I mailed the letters, I'd stop in at the Ritz every few days on my lunch hour to collect the answers.

Now it's one thing to sound like a haughty noblewoman on paper, and quite another to look it. I didn't look it. I had a dumpy little figure and the clothes I bought off the sale racks in Wanamaker's basement didn't improve it. I had straight mouse-colored hair which I couldn't afford to have cut or set very often, I wore glasses, and I had as much poise as any young girl who's never been anywhere or done anything and most of the time isn't exactly sure who she is.

Thus equipped, I had to lope up to the Ritz-Carlton desk, tell the clerk I was Baroness von Hanff and ask for my mail. This so unnerved me it was a positive pleasure to get back to the office and work on my current second act through a two-hour saxophone lesson.

That's where I was working when, on a Friday early in February, the letter came. My father and my two older brothers all got home from work that evening before I did. I walked into the living room and found the whole family gathered in awed silence around a white envelope that lay on our wobbly marble-topped coffee table. My mother handed me the letter. On the back of the envelope was the printed legend, HOTEL DORSET, NEW YORK CITY. Above this was written in ink, "Theresa Helburn."

I stared at it and my knees went weak. I sat down abruptly on the worn blue sofa and stared round at my parents and my brothers, and still nobody spoke. Nothing so momentous had ever happened in our family.

Both my parents were passionate theatregoers. My father in his youth had run away from college to go on the stage as a song-and-dance man. His show-business career lasted only two years. He got stranded in Montana and wired home for money, and my grandmother sent him a train ticket instead.

"When he came home," my mother told me, "he had lice or something, and your grandmother threw him into the bathtub, burned all his clothes, and told him he was through with the theatre."

So he became a shirt salesman, married my mother and settled down. But Philadelphia was a favorite tryout city for Broadway plays, and my father spent the rest of his life swapping shirts for passes with all the box-office men in Philadelphia. This was an ideal arrangement in the thirties because box-office men had too many empty theatre seats and not enough shirts. So throughout the Depression, though the taxes on our house weren't paid or the installments on the old secondhand car, and though the prescription for my mother's new glasses went unfilled, every Monday night our whole family went to theatre.

We always brought a program home, to be pasted in the Theatre Book, a large album in which my parents kept the program of every show they saw, each program marked with a pencilled letter in the upper right-hand corner: E, G, F, or R. E for Excellent, G for Good, F for Fair, R for Rotten. On rainy evenings, my brothers pored over the book, scanning the cast lists of 1920s plays for the names of bit players who had since become Hollywood stars: Humphrey Bogart, Bette Davis, Barbara Stanwyck. But in our house such names never carried the weight of genuine theatre names — Shaw and the Lunts, Noel Coward and O'Neill.

To my parents, the theatre was a large, many-mansioned religion. The *sanctum sanctorum* of this religion was the Theatre Guild, then presided over by its co-producers, Theresa Helburn and Lawrence Langner. The Theatre Guild was the most prestigious of producing organizations, celebrated for its lofty dedication to the theatre as Art. Even my brothers, though agnostic as they grew older, had been firmly reared in this faith and, like my parents, regarded the Guild with awe. Now here they all were, contemplating a letter from the High Priestess herself — addressed to Sis. I come of a noisy family, and never before or after were they so quiet as when they watched me open that letter.

"Dear Miss Hanff," it read. "I am interested in your work. Can you come to New York to lunch with me on Tuesday? I enclose the fare."

Enclosed was a check for five dollars.

During dinner we all shouted happily at each other that the Bureau of New Plays must be the Theatre Guild in disguise and Terry Helburn must be the contest judge and wouldn't she be pleased to learn my family never missed a Theatre Guild production.

I went through the weekend in a fog. On Monday, I showed the letter to my two bosses, who said I could have Tuesday off. All day Monday I worried about what to wear, and wished I had the money to have my hair done.

On Monday night, my father triumphantly brought home for me a new green rayon suit which he had got wholesale from a friend. The suit was a brighter green than I would have chosen, and not precisely my size, but my mother took it in at the waist and let it out at the hips and cut off the row of threads that hung from the hem, and we decided it looked great.

On Tuesday morning, wearing my old blue winter coat with the grey fur collar over the new green suit, I boarded the train for New York armed with a round-trip ticket and enough money for a cab to the Hotel Dorset.

It was an ostentatiously quiet residential hotel with an elegantly uniformed doorman. But if you had a personal appointment with Theresa Helburn you were not to be intimidated by a doorman. Reeking with poise, I sailed grandly past him into the plush lobby and up to the desk and informed the lady behind it that I wished to see Miss Theresa Helburn.

"She's expecting me," I added graciously.

The desk clerk looked surprised.

"I don't think she's here," she said. "I think she moved out."

My *sangfroid* evaporated.

"She must be here!" I said in a high-pitched bleat. "She wrote to me on your stationery!"

I showed the lady my envelope with HOTEL DORSET and "Theresa Helburn" on the back. She nodded pleasantly but without conviction.

"Just a minute, I'll see," she said, and disappeared into a small office beyond the desk. Then she came back.

"Miss Helburn moved out," she said. "Try the Warwick." And she turned away to greet a pair of mink-clad arrivals.

I left the lobby and went out to the sidewalk and stood there in a panic. I didn't know where the Warwick was; I didn't have money for another cab so I'd have to find it by bus or on foot, with no guarantee Theresa Helburn would be there when I found it.

The Dorset doorman must have sensed the commotion in me because he bowed in courtly fashion and asked if he might be of assistance.

"I'm looking for Miss Theresa Helburn," I quavered. "She wrote and told me to meet her here, and now they say she's moved out, and I know if she moved she'd have let me know!"

Once more I produced my envelope. The doorman raised an arm and pointed a forefinger at a residential hotel directly across the street.

"She moved back to the Warwick," he said. Then he leaned down and whispered conspiratorially: "Flop!"

"Pardon?" I said.

"Miss Helburn lives at the Warwick," he explained. "But when the Guild has too many flops in a row she decides the Warwick is bringing her bad luck and she moves over here to us."

"Doesn't she have flops here?" I asked.

"Oh, yes," he said. "Then she moves back to the Warwick." He gave me a prodigious wink. "You go on over there; you'll find her."

So I went across the street to the Warwick and through another elegant lobby to the desk and asked the desk clerk tensely whether Miss Helburn was registered. And when he said he'd ring her suite, relief flooded through me.

While he rang, I watched the parade of glamorous people through the lobby. It was almost one o'clock, and sleekly beautiful women buried in furs were on their way to the dining room, where they were met by full-chested, middle-aged men. I became conscious of my old blue coat and took it off and draped it over my arm to let my new suit show.

The desk clerk gave me a suite number and told me to go right up. I was the only passenger in the elevator, and now that I was actually going to come face to face with Theresa Helburn my heart pounded so loudly I was afraid the elevator operator would hear it. He let me out at the tenth floor and I went down the long carpeted hall to a door at the end and pressed the bell. Chimes rang mellowly inside, and I hoped it would be a maid instead of a butler who opened the door, but I straightened to my full five-feet-three and prepared to deal with either.

Terry herself opened the door, and I gawked at her: she was barely five feet tall, making me feel suddenly large. She had short, fluffy white hair, bright blue eyes, a blunt square nose and a blunt square chin — and awed though I was, she reminded me then and ever after of a shrewd, friendly toy bulldog.

"Hello, dear," she said. "Come in. Give me your coat."

I stepped into the spacious, impersonal hotel living room, and Terry took my coat and waved around at a sofa and a couple of armchairs and said:

"Sit down, dear."

Being awkward as well as nearsighted, I lunged at the nearest armchair and tripped over what appeared to be a grey-and-white fur coat lying on the floor beside it — whereat the grey-and-white fur coat rose to its four feet with a mildly indignant bass bark.

"Go away, Blunder, and sit down somewhere," Terry advised the fur coat. Blunder was one of those mammoth, improbable Old English sheepdogs with a face so immersed in shaggy fur you had to guess where his eyes were. I sat down in the armchair and Blunder walked off to the middle of the rug and sat down facing me.

"When I bought him," said Terry, "everybody called him 'Terry's blunder' so that's what I named him. I'll put some lipstick on and we'll go down to the dining room."

She went off to the bedroom and I got up and stole a look in the mirror over the sofa. My hair needed combing, my skirt had acquired a thousand small, knifelike creases, and a whole new crop of threads had sprouted from the hem. I didn't have a comb, I didn't have scissors and I didn't have nerve enough to ask for either. I sat back down, very low in my mind, and the sight of my unhappy face obviously moved Blunder because he got up, walked over to me, put his massive front paws on my shoulders and gave me a broad, wet kiss.

Terry meanwhile was calling questions about my education, job and taste in plays. While I answered, Blunder got as much of himself onto my lap as would fit, kissing me in a transport of enthusiasm which removed the last vestiges of powder and lipstick.

And so, as I trailed Terry into the Warwick dining room, past a gantlet of chic women who called to her from every table, my green suit with the threads hanging from it was covered evenly from shoulder to hem with grey-white sheepdog hair.

Terry sailed to a back table where, she said, we could talk in peace. A waiter brought imposing menus, and Terry, after studying her menu for a minute and me for another minute, announced I was too young to drink in the middle of the day and advised me to try the creamed chicken. The ordering thus disposed of, she got down to business.

"Your plays are terrible," she told me, beaming. "Just terrible!" And she laughed. "Never mind. You have talent."

She told me the Bureau of New Plays was financed by several Hollywood studios and that she herself had nothing to do with the contest, though the Guild "might do something for the winners."

"I lent them my secretary as a playreader," she said, "and when she finds a script she thinks shows talent, she steals it for me." She grinned at me. "I've got all four of your plays, but the judges don't know it. I'll put them back when I'm through with them."

Lunch arrived and she stared at the creamed chicken and then allowed that Play No. 4 wasn't as bad as the others and after lunch she'd show me how to rewrite it. Then she asked whether I planned to change my name. I said it hadn't occurred to me. For the next ten minutes, between bites of her chicken, Terry repeated my name aloud ten or twelve times, with varying inflections. Then she nodded decisively.

"Keep it," she said. "If anybody ever gets it straight, they'll remember it."

After coffee, we went back up to her suite where she worked all afternoon with me reconstructing Play No. 4. When I left her at five, she said:

"Bring me the first-act revisions next Tuesday. If you don't have the fare, borrow it from your parents and I'll reimburse you. And bring me a copy of the play for myself so I can put this one back."

She told me which Fifth Avenue bus would take me to Penn Station and I floated home to Philadelphia.

For the next six weeks, from early February to mid-March, I went to see Terry every Tuesday. My two bosses had to close their office and go their separate ways so I was out of work again, but Terry said it was just as well because I needed to study. She had me buy Aristotle's *Poetics* and Stanislavski's *My Life in Art* and *An Actor Prepares* and Lawson's *Theory and Technique of Playwriting* and quizzed me on certain key passages in each to make sure I understood them.

The Broadway season was then at its height. Terry was looking in on rehearsals of a new Guild play, she was overseeing the road company production of another play about to tour the Guild's subscription cities, and she was working with two authors whose plays the Guild had under option. All afternoon every Tuesday as we worked, the phone rang, the desk sent up importunate messages from stars, agents, directors, and Terry's harassed secretary hurried in and out with reminders of auditions and backers' conferences and memos on contracts and run-throughs, vainly trying to keep Terry from wasting the whole afternoon on me. And week after week, Terry went on wasting it.

The Tuesday before March 15 — when the contest winners were to be announced — she said to me over lunch:

"I don't know what three names the judges have picked, dear, but if you're not one of the winners don't worry about it. I can take care of you."

And I was so moved I couldn't even thank her, I just nodded dumbly. At dinner that night, I explained airily to my family that I really didn't care whether I won a fellowship or not.

Which was a good thing because March 13 and 14 came and went, with no word from the Bureau of New Plays. Since the winners were to go on the radio to accept their fellowships at a ceremonial dinner on the fifteenth, I thought it unlikely that word would come as late as that morning. And sure enough, nothing came in the mail on the morning of the fifteenth.

In spite of Terry's warning, I was disappointed. To console myself, I went downtown and shopped for a spring outfit to wear-to-New-York-on-Tuesdays. I bought a navy suit with a white collar and navy shoes and bag, but it took me all day since the less you have to spend the longer it takes you to find what you want. So it was five o'clock when, lugging my bundles, I turned the corner of our block, started up the street toward our house — and stopped in my tracks.

Camped on our doorstep were half a dozen reporters and photographers talking to my mother. She saw me and beckoned frantically, and I loped into a run, bundles flapping.

"Miss Helburn's on the phone," my mother called as I came within earshot. "She wants to know where you are."

I ran up the front steps and into the house, my mother following and the press bringing up the rear.

"You won," my mother said. "You're the only girl. You're the youngest. The newspapers got a telegram."

I picked up the phone and said hello, but Terry had hung up. Feeling lightheaded, I sat down to be interviewed and photographed. Just as the press was leaving, the phone rang again and I hurried to answer it.

"Why aren't you in New York?" Terry demanded. "You go on the air at seven-forty-five!"

"I just found out about it!" I said. "I wasn't notified. I didn't get a letter or a telegram or anything!"

"Well, you knew you won," said Terry. "You've been seeing me for weeks."

It was no time to answer: "But you said —." I changed into the new blue suit, took the next train to New York and went on the radio with the other two winners to accept the fellowship. Two months later, Terry took me to Westport, Connecticut, to work as an apprentice at the Guild's summer theatre; and in the fall I moved to New York on my fellowship money, having been enrolled by Terry in a playwriting seminar to be conducted by the Theatre Guild.

And since nobody had told me about Flanagan's Law, I didn't realize that with a start like that, I was positively certain to get nowhere at all in the theatre.

Footnote to Chapter 1:
It Doesn't Pay
to Educate Playwrights

BEFORE I'D BEEN IN NEW YORK a month, I made the shocked discovery that most people who worked in the theatre made fun of the Theatre Guild. You mentioned the Guild at Sardi's (shyly and proudly) and everybody died laughing.

What baffled me about this was that the laughers included the stars and playwrights, directors and designers who were most impressed by the Guild's artistic standards and most eager to be involved in Guild productions.

Then what was so funny?

Consider the saga of the Bureau of New Plays and its fellowship winners, and the playwriting seminar the Guild conducted for them. It was the sort of high-minded fiasco that could have happened only to the Theatre Guild.

The Bureau of New Plays had been founded one year earlier and had awarded two fellowships that year, giving the winners $1,500 each and sending them on their way. During the second year, when I was one of the winners, the Theatre Guild stepped in.

"You're doing this all wrong," said the Theatre Guild to the Bureau of New Plays. "It's a great mistake to give young writers money and send them wandering off on their own. Playwrights need training! So this year," finished the Theatre Guild, "you give them the money and we'll give them the training."

Having hatched this lofty and commendable project, the Guild rounded up twelve promising young playwrights and enrolled us in a seminar. The Guild had its own building and theatre on West Fifty-second Street, and on a mild September afternoon we gathered in the third-floor board room for our first session, to be conducted by Lawrence Langner and Terry, the Guild's co-producers.

At first glance, it was a typical board room, large and quiet, with wide windows and a polished mahogany board table long enough to seat all of us. What gave the room its quality, and awed us into silence as we took our places at the table, were the faces that looked down at us from massively framed photographs on the walls.

There was Shaw, with a pixie smile and a note scrawled across the beard. There was O'Neill, staring somberly into space, the Lunts in a flamboyant scene from *The Taming of the Shrew*, Maurice Evans as Falstaff, and Ethel Barrymore and Gertie Lawrence, and George Gershwin with the original cast of *Porgy and Bess*.

The hallowed history of the Theatre Guild flowed out from those walls as Lawrence Langner looked into our solemn faces and told us the future of the theatre rested with us. Terry added her own welcome and then Lawrence outlined the seminar.

We were to meet in the board room three afternoons a week, in classes to be taught by producer Cheryl Crawford, director Lee Strasberg, and Guild playreader John Gassner. Occasionally Terry or Lawrence would lecture on production, and from time to time famous actors, actresses, playwrights and directors would be brought in as guest lecturers.

In addition, each student would attend morning rehearsals of a new Broadway play. There were several new plays to be produced by the Guild. Cheryl Crawford was also producing one; Lee Strasberg was directing one; and John Gassner had written one. Each of us was to be assigned to rehearsals of one of these productions. We would also be given tickets to Broadway plays. Thus began the education of twelve young would-be playwrights, an intensive professional training the luckless winners of the previous year's fellowships might well have envied. Nothing was overlooked, no time or trouble was spared; and in March, when the seminar ended, everybody agreed it had been a great success.

There was, to be sure, one small hitch. We had attended rehearsals of our mentors' productions so that we might study and analyze the best new plays, those which had met the high standards of the Theatre Guild.

The play produced by Guild protégée Cheryl Crawford flopped.

The play written by Guild playreader John Gassner flopped.

The play directed by Lee Strasberg flopped.

All four plays produced by the Theatre Guild flopped.

But that's a detail. The worth of the seminar itself can fairly be judged only by the ultimate achievements of the twelve neophyte playwrights so carefully educated. What became of them?

One — Danny Taradash — became a screenwriter with an Academy Award to his credit. A second — John Crosby — became a famous TV critic.

No. 3 became a physician, No. 4 is a short-story writer, No. 5 manages a movie theatre, Nos. 6 and 7 are English professors, Nos. 8 and 9 became TV writers, Nos. 10 and 11 became screenwriters, and No. 12 has a private income and seems not to have done much of anything. (You'll find out soon enough which of these I was.)

The Theatre Guild, convinced that fledgling playwrights need training as well as money, exhausted itself training twelve of us —

and not one of the twelve ever became a Broadway playwright. The two fellowship winners who, the previous year, had been given $1,500 and sent wandering off on their own were Tennessee Williams and Arthur Miller.

·2·

"No Casting Today But Keep in Touch!"

WHEN MAXINE AND I MET and became best friends — in the back-stage ladies' room of the Morosco Theatre — I thought she was the most glamorous creature on earth. Maxine was a bona fide Broadway actress.

We met during my fellowship winter when I was assigned to rehearsals of a comedy called *Yankee Fable,* in which Maxine had an impressively large role as the comedy-ingenue — impressive to me because Maxine was my own age. Sitting in the dark, empty theatre during the first two days of rehearsal, I had gawked more at the redheaded comedy-ingenue than at the star. It awed me that someone as young as I was should be so poised and assured and so thoroughly at home on a Broadway stage as Maxine was.

On the third day, I went into the backstage ladies' room to wash before lunch, and the redhead was standing at the sink. She was fussing with the straps under the shoulders of her white silk blouse, and when she saw me she turned beet-red. I smiled uncertainly, wondering what she was blushing at.

"Have you got a safety pin?" she asked.

"No, I don't," I mumbled, tongue-tied in the presence of so much glamour. She turned away and went on fussing with the brassiere straps or whatever they were, and as I washed my hands I goggled at her covertly, never having seen a real actress at such close range. Maxine had the kind of beauty people goggled at anyway. She had thick masses of hair the color of flaming autumn leaves that curled about her face in loose ringlets, a complexion like milk and one of those swan necks you see in 1890s portraits. It was when I had got as far as her neck that I noticed something peculiar below it. Maxine's left breast appeared to be a couple of inches higher than her right.

She saw my puzzled stare and her eyes suddenly filled with tears.

"What's the matter?" I asked.

"It's my damn falsies," she said. "I can't get them to stay put."

"Can't you take them off?" I asked timidly.

"How can I go back onstage with no bosoms when I had them all morning?" she demanded. "Everybody would notice!"

"Oh, I don't think they would," I said earnestly. "Listen, I've been watching you all morning. Why don't you take them off and walk up and down, and I'll tell you if I notice the difference."

Maxine removed the falsies, buttoned her white blouse, threw her shoulders back and walked away a few steps to give me a profile view. Then she turned and faced me bravely.

"Nobody," I stated positively, "will notice a thing! You don't need falsies, you have a lovely figure!"

"I'm playing a sexy part, I wouldn't have got it if they'd known I was flat-chested," said Maxine.

"You're wonderful in the part!" I said. "They hired you for your talent, not your bust!"

"I nearly died when I felt them slip during the last scene," she said, wrapping the falsies carefully in Kleenex and putting them in her handbag. "I'm nervous enough in this company. They're all such pros."

"Well, you're a pro!" I said.

Maxine giggled.

"I only graduated from the American Academy last June," she said. "The Guild took me out of the senior class and gave me my first job and when the show closed I went back and graduated. This is only my second show."

"You must be terrific, if you made the American Academy of Dramatic Art and then got taken out of the senior class by the Theatre Guild!" I said. And I added, trying to sound offhand about it: "You know, it's funny: I'm a Theatre Guild protégée, too."

"I know," said Maxine. "I asked somebody who you were because nobody else in the company is my age, and they said you were a playwright sent over by the Guild. That's why I never had the nerve to talk to you."

She saw the uncomprehending look on my face and explained: "People with brains intimidate me." And she added simply, "I don't have any brains."

I laughed. I think I knew that people who really have no brains don't know it. And having read my Stanislavski, I knew that acting demanded a high degree of intelligence. But I understood what she meant: we both grew up equating brains with college degrees.

"I don't have any brains either! I only went to college for one year," I assured her. "I don't even know anything about the theatre and you're a professional Broadway actress!"

"My name's Maxine Stuart," she said. "Have you got a lunch date?"

So we went to lunch together at Ralph's, an Eighth Avenue restaurant patronized exclusively by the 999 theatre hopefuls who couldn't afford Sardi's.

After that, we exchanged daily confidences in the backstage ladies' room under a large daisy-sprinkled wall poster that assured us "Syphilis CAN Be Cured!" By the end of *Yankee Fable*'s three weeks of rehearsal, I was firmly convinced Maxine was a finer comedienne than the show's star and she had read my latest play and pronounced it far superior to *Yankee Fable*. Damon and Pythias had met.

Yankee Fable went to Washington, D.C., for the usual two-week out-of-town tryout. It opened in Washington, closed in Washington and died in Washington. In two weeks, therefore, Maxine was back home living the normal everyday life of a glamorous young actress.

A young actress engages in three kinds of activity. First, there's physical training. An actress has to train everything from her vocal cords to her toe muscles, so that her body — known to Stanislavski disciples as her Instrument — will be in perfect condition for her life onstage. Second, there's "making the rounds": paying daily or twice-weekly visits to the offices of producers rumored to be casting new shows, interspersed — not often enough — with auditions for producers and casting directors. Third, and rarest, there's the glorious achievement: rehearsing and appearing in a Broadway play.

I first learned about Maxine's method of training her Instrument on the Sunday after *Yankee Fable* died in Washington when Maxine invited me to her house for lunch.

Maxine lived with her parents in a big, comfortable apartment on West End Avenue, and in no time at all that apartment became my second home. Maxine's parents were a short, plump, benign middle-class couple comfortingly like my own parents. They knew I lived in a furnished room and ate my meals in the nearest cafeteria, and being warm-hearted people they got themselves rapidly trapped into feeding me oftener than the cafeteria did.

Maxine's mother opened the door to me at noon that Sunday. Beyond her I could see Maxine's father stretched out on the sofa with the Sunday *Times*. As I opened my mouth to say hello to both of them, there was a piercing scream from the bathroom down the hall.

"Oh, NO!" screamed Maxine, the "NO" turning into a long, blood-curdling wail that raised the hair on my scalp.

"Did you have any breakfast, dear?" Maxine's mother asked,

musical, I began to sing one of the songs from it under my breath. Maxine joined in, in her authoritative, resonant voice, and after two bars I stopped and stared at her.

"You're singing it all on one note!" I said.

"I know," said Maxine. "I can't carry a tune."

I don't know how many singing teachers wore themselves out trying to teach Maxine to carry a tune. None of them ever succeeded. Which was unfortunate, because producers assume that any actress can sing passably enough to manage the refrain of a popular song if a scene in a play happens to call for it.

So a procession of vocal coaches worked long and hard before they abandoned their efforts to teach Maxine to sing and, instead, taught her to manipulate her speaking voice and project it in a large theatre. With phenomenal results: Maxine's powers of projection were such that she could turn to me, in the first balcony of Loew's Eighty-third Street movie theatre, and whisper:

"Do you think it's safe to use the ladies' room here? I have to go," and be heard clearly by everybody sitting below us on the orchestra floor and above us in the second balcony, not to mention the people on our own level who turned to stare at us from rows around.

Then there were dancing lessons. In pursuit of that grace and lightness necessary to the perfection of her Instrument, Maxine decided to take up ballet. For a whole year, we took ballet lessons from a Greek who taught us a little Greek classic dancing on the side. I went along, partly because Maxine said it would tone up my system, but mostly because I was studying Greek at the time and had visions of carrying on chatty conversations with the ballet teacher in beginner's ancient Greek.

(Studying Greek was one of the things I was doing to perfect *my* Instrument. My Instrument was the English language — and since the English language derives so largely from Latin and Greek, how could I hope to select the precisely right English word every time I wrote one, if I didn't know the Greek or Latin root of every word in the language? as I explained impressively to Maxine.)

Every morning after she trained her Instrument, Maxine prepared for her second activity — making the rounds — by spending a painstaking hour applying street makeup. First she pencilled feathery brown eyebrows over the pale pink ones God had thoughtlessly given her. Then she overlaid her pale pink eyelashes with feathery brown mascara. Next came rouge and lipstick, each chosen with no more care than the average girl would spend in choosing her wedding dress; and finally face powder, dusted on and then carefully brushed off. When her makeup was complete, Maxine looked as if she were wearing no makeup at all. This job done, she climbed into high heels and a chic suit and was off on her rounds of producers' and agents' offices.

In every one of these offices, there was a sign on the wall saying, *No casting today. Please leave your name;* or, more cheerily, *No casting today but keep in touch!* You could walk into the office of a producer who was casting a new musical, and find a horde of young actors and actresses who'd been summoned to audition overflowing the sofas, chairs and windowsills till late arrivals had to sit cross-legged on the floor, and above them on the wall a large sign stubbornly insisted, *No casting today.* The signs were like pictures; they were never taken down.

So kids making the rounds learned to ignore them. They also devised ingenious methods for forcing the attention of the receptionist in the producer's outer office, who was usually the only person they were permitted to see. Say you were a young actor or actress making the rounds and you walked into the office of a producer who was casting a new play. You stepped up to the desk and asked politely if you might see the producer.

"No-casting-today," said the receptionist in a bored tone and without looking up. "If-you-want-to-leave-your-name —" And her pencil moved to a pad, but she still didn't look up. This was very frustrating because you might have heard you were exactly the physical type the producer was looking for, and how could the receptionist know this if she didn't look at you? So you invented a trick to force her to focus on you. Bill Flanagan of Flanagan's Law, for instance, changed his first name to Brazelius and added the initial P. when he made the rounds.

"She asks you to leave your name," he explained to me, "and if you say 'Bill Flanagan' she writes it down without looking up. But if you say 'Brazelius P. Flanagan' she looks up. She asks you how to spell it, she stares at you to see if you're serious — and she remembers the name later."

He claimed he got a lot of work on the strength of that Brazelius. Of course, when he signed a contract, he reverted to Bill.

Maxine's trick was not to answer when a receptionist asked her name.

"You-wanta-leave-your-name?" the receptionist would mumble, pencil poised above her writing pad, eyes on her manicure. Maxine would stand silent until the receptionist was finally forced to look up to see if she was still there. Once the receptionist looked up, she saw Maxine's mop of flaming red hair, which was dramatic enough to be remembered.

Having made the rounds of producers' and agents' offices faithfully, Maxine was regularly rewarded by being asked to audition for some new Broadway play. Those auditions not only aged her parents considerably and ruined their digestion and mine; they also conformed to Flanagan's Law by simply defying expectation.

Take, for example, the afternoon when an agent named Eddie sent for Maxine to tell her she was to audition the next morning for the producer and director of what promised to be the new season's outstanding production. The playwright was famous, the two stars were internationally known, the director was the most sought-after. The cast was set except for the comedy-ingenue.

"You are so right for the part," said Eddie, "that after they've seen you I don't think they'll bother to hear anybody else read for it! Provided" — and he paused solemnly — "provided — you give the best damn audition you've ever given. This is a top-drawer production, dear. I don't want to send you over there unless you feel you can give a top-drawer reading."

Now in the best of times and under tranquil conditions, Maxine was by nature highly emotional. (We were both by nature highly emotional.) Under the conditions Eddie had created, she was Joan of Arc and *The Snake Pit* combined.

She phoned me that evening and, with death in her voice, asked me to come to her at once; she couldn't stand to be alone and she couldn't stand to be with her parents and she was feeling nauseous and so forth. I hurried up to West End Avenue, arriving just as Maxine's parents were leaving for the movies (I gathered they couldn't stand to be with her either), and Maxine's mother, looking careworn, said:

"She's in her room, dear. You'd better knock."

I went down the hall and knocked timidly on Maxine's bed-room door. When she opened it, I said, "Hiya" hollowly, took off my coat and hat and dropped them on the bed — and Maxine promptly had hysterics. That's how I found out it was bad luck in the theatre to put hats on beds.

When we both stopped crying I asked her what kind of temperament the role called for.

"I don't know," said Maxine coldly. "It's a secret! I don't know whether to look ingenue or sexy or sophisticated. First Eddie says I'm exactly right for the part, now he admits he hasn't seen the script! Nobody's seen the script!"

She plucked an invisible eyebrow and glared at me in the mirror, her brown eyes snapping with fury.

". . . incredible people, they have the bloody play MIMEO-graphed and then they dig a hole under the subway and BURY all five hundred copies, God forbid anybody who's going to audition for it should *read* it!"

"What else has Eddie sent you out for?" I asked. "What type does he think you are?"

The tweezer froze in Maxine's hand. She stood a moment in the attitude of one listening to the distant roll of the tumbrel. And she whispered in horror:

"I'm coming down with a cold."

In Maxine's life this was the overriding catastrophe. A cold ruined you, it ruined your looks, your resonance, your projection, everything.

"It's not a cold, it's just nerves," I said.

"There's a prickle in the back of my throat, I'm getting a cold!" She went out to the kitchen and heated a kettle of water and draped a towel over her head and spent the rest of the evening steaming her sinuses while we discussed what she should wear to the audition, what material she should use if they asked her to do her own material, and whether she should tell the blonde star that redheads look very well under pink lights so the star wouldn't veto her as interfering with blonde lighting.

At midnight, when I left her, she was icily calm. She stood in the doorway in her blue bathrobe and bare feet, her fiery hair stuck up in curlers, her nose slathered with freckle cream and her face beet-red from the long steaming, and said in a remote voice:

"I may not call you tomorrow. I know definitely now I'm going to give a ghastly audition."

"You're going to give a wonderful audition," I said.

We were both wrong. You were always wrong. You persisted in assuming there were two possibilities and there were always three: the two you thought of and the one that happened.

Maxine arrived at the producer's office and the secretary ushered her into an inner office where four men were waiting for her: producer, director, author, casting director. One sat behind the desk, one was in an armchair, the other two were on the sofa. Having announced Maxine's name, the secretary withdrew, leaving Maxine standing alone in the middle of the room.

The four men stared at her. Nobody spoke. Nobody asked her to sit down, nobody introduced himself, nobody asked her to read.

The silence lasted for several minutes during which they went on staring at her. Finally, one of the men spoke.

"I don't see it," he said.

"I told Eddie what we wanted!" (That was the casting director.)

"I don't see this at all," the third man agreed. The fourth man said nothing. He had a hangnail and he was working on it. The first man pressed a buzzer and the secretary appeared. Looking past Maxine as if she didn't exist, the first man said to the secretary:

"Who else is out there?" The secretary named another young actress, and the producer said: "All right, send her in."

The secretary ushered Maxine out. The audition was over. Maxine met me for lunch afterward at the Astor Drugstore, which was a theatre kids' hangout, and she had even the countermen clutching the walls for support as she acted out the audition for everybody.

There were auditions where she walked out on stage to read and was stopped before she opened her mouth because she was too tall, or too short, for her scene with the leading man. There were auditions where they decided they didn't want a redhead or had thought she was British.

And there was the winter when she was in Florida with a stock company and got a telegram from an agent saying CAN YOU FLY UP SUNDAY IMPORTANT AUDITION MONDAY MORNING and she flew up and phoned the agent and discovered she was to audition for the New Opera Company.

Nothing daunted, she went out on the New Opera Company stage and did her best comedy material, after which the fat little director came hurtling down the aisle crying:

"Magnificent, liebchen, absolutely perfect for ze part! Now let's hear you zing zomezing."

Boom. Don't-call-us-we'll-call-you.

Never mind. Once a year came the audition when she actually

got the part; and on that day, my friend Maxine owned the earth. She sailed down Fifth Avenue or floated up Broadway in a radiant glow that caused people to stare after her, bemused. Or, as one of her beaux observed to me with a wistful sigh (he wasn't in the theatre):

"Maxine with a job is like any other woman in love."

Of course, after the successful audition came the first five days of rehearsal during which Maxine and her parents and I all lived in a permanent state of acid indigestion because during the first five days of rehearsal, an actress could be fired. Not till the sixth day was she given a contract. I spent the five probationary evenings cueing Maxine in her lines (while she steamed her sinuses) and saying hello and good-bye to her parents who went off nightly to the movies looking more and more careworn.

From the day she signed the contract, there was nothing more to worry about till the night before the opening when pre-opening night nerves set in. At 11 P.M. on the night before one opening, she threw the New York telephone directory at me (I can't lift it myself without using both hands), whereupon I stalked off and went huffily home to bed, to be awakened at 1 A.M. by the telephone conveying weeping apologies from West End Avenue. (Such evenings consoled me for what I put Maxine through when I was out of work and no producer would buy my play, which was most of the time.)

On opening nights, Maxine's parents were lucky: they weren't allowed to go; they might make her nervous. They went on the second night when the crisis was past.

I was allowed to go to the opening. I sat through each one with my stomach churning and all my fingers crossed. Maxine never gave a bad opening-night performance, but most of the plays she appeared in were the kind of total flops we referred to as "dawgs." I'd sit through the three acts gamely and, as soon as the final curtain fell, hurry backstage to Maxine's dressing room and say the wrong thing.

An actor I knew did a very funny act at parties in which he mimicked the well-meaning friends who always came backstage after an opening to offer foot-in-mouth congratulations. The funniest bit in his act mortified me because it was what I invariably said to Maxine after every one of her openings. I'd hurry backstage, knowing the play was a dawg that wouldn't last a week, walk into Maxine's dressing room and say earnestly:

"*I* LIKED it! I really did!"

If you can't do better than that, just leave a note with the stage doorman telling your friend she was sensational and go on home.

Maxine appeared in eleven Broadway plays, most of which opened on a Tuesday night. On Wednesday came the flop notices, on Thursday an empty house, on Friday the closing notice went up, on Saturday the show closed and on Sunday Maxine slept it off.

And so, on Monday, she was once more to be found in her parents' apartment on West End Avenue ready to resume the normal daily life of a glamorous young actress by screaming "Oh, NO!" in the bathroom.

·3·

If They Take You to Lunch They Don't Want Your Play

WHEN A YOUNG PLAYWRIGHT — temporarily starved out of New York and back in the bosom of her family in Philadelphia — receives two phone calls from two Broadway producers in the same afternoon, and each producer says: "You've written a wonderful play. When can you come to New York to see me?" the playwright naturally assumes that both producers want to produce her play.

Not until she has hurried off to New York and seen both producers and been left stranded at Penn Station at three in the morning with thirty-five cents and her play unsold does it occur to her that there must have been a flaw in her thinking. Somehow or other, she has failed to understand how producers' minds work.

The phone calls came on a Tuesday in March, a month after I'd gone home for a second wind. I'd hung on in New York for a couple of years after my fellowship year ended, keeping alive on dreary office jobs, from which I was regularly fired for typing my plays on company time. That February, I'd lost the one job too many and when my capital had shrunk to the price of a one-way ticket to Philadelphia, I'd packed my bags, left a new play at my agent's office, said a tearful good-bye to Maxine and crept mournfully home.

The first of the two calls came early in the afternoon as I was trying to get a whole cigarette out of my brother.

My oldest brother was married by then but the middle one was still living at home. I wouldn't say he was exactly working at the time, but he was earning money, which I wasn't. (He later became a big wheel in industry so I'm not allowed to say that his earnings came from playing pool and duplicate bridge in local contests. He was so expert at both games that rich men backed him, won heavily on him and gave him a percentage of their winnings.)

Since my parents were feeding and housing me, I didn't need cash for anything but cigarettes and these my father generally remembered to buy for me. It was when he forgot that I was forced to appeal to my brother's better nature — such as it was. I'd ask him for a cigarette and he'd ponder the request.

"I'd be glad to give you one," he'd say earnestly, "but one cigarette won't help you. You'll smoke it — and in half an hour you'll be out of cigarettes again. Now what I'd like to do is find a way to give you enough cigarettes to last you awhile."

He'd take six or seven cigarettes out of his pack, hold them half-out to me and ponder them. And the minute I reached for one, he'd yank them back and say:

"I know how to do it!"

And he'd take a penknife out of his pocket, cut all six or seven cigarettes in half, and hand me the butts thus accumulated. This was before king-size cigarettes had come on the market, so you know how long half a cigarette was. You couldn't light it without burning your upper lip and the tip of your nose.

I did not stand idly by while he mutilated six cigarettes. But it's very difficult for a girl to get cigarettes by force from a brother who's bigger and taller than she is and has an open penknife in one hand. So as I said, I was trying to appeal to his better nature when the phone rang.

"Miss Hanff?" said a woman's voice at the other end. "Just a moment, please. Oscar Serlin calling from New York."

All the blood left my head. Oscar Serlin had produced *Life With Father*, then in its fourth or fifth year on Broadway and with road companies across the country, including one in Philadelphia that was breaking records there in its second year. Of all Broadway hits, this had been the biggest.

"Miss Hanff?" said Oscar Serlin in a deep baritone voice. "I've read your play. I'm very impressed. When can you come to New York to see me?"

We settled on Friday afternoon and when I hung up I was shaking. I managed to tell my brother the news and he was so impressed he gave me a whole cigarette. I'd only just finished it when the second call came. This one was from a producer we'll call Charlie. He also had a play running on Broadway. It had got mixed reviews but it had been running since early October and was by no means a flop. Said Charlie, without reservation or preamble:

"I think you've written a marvelous play. I want to produce it."

He went on for half an hour about the characters and the dialogue, which he said were both marvelous, and about the theme of the play which was also marvelous.

"I have some friends who are interested in it and we all want to meet you," he said. "When can I give a small dinner party for you?"

I said I was coming to New York on Friday and Charlie said Friday evening would be ideal for the dinner party. He gave me his address and told me again how marvelous the play was and we hung up. I phoned my agent, who congratulated me and ordered me not to set foot in either producer's lair until I'd seen her first.

On Friday, wearing my good spring suit and carrying a new silk blouse (charged to my mother on my prospects) to change into for the dinner party, I set out for New York, with the fare donated by my father, and a nearly full pack of cigarettes and fifty cents for buses donated by my brother.

Hoarding the fifty cents for emergencies, I walked from Penn Station to my agent's office. She welcomed me warmly and gave me instructions. Oscar Serlin, she said, was one of Broadway's most discriminating producers and I was to let him have the play. However, I was to be very, very nice to Charlie because, while she didn't think too highly of his current production, one simply never knew what next year might bring.

I phoned Maxine from my agent's office and told her the news. She was in rehearsal for one of the bombs she was periodically cast in and we shrieked congratulations at each other over the phone.

"Listen, I'll be home all evening," she said. "Call me and tell me what happened!"

"I'll phone you before I leave town," I promised. And wouldn't I just.

I left my agent's office and went around the corner to Oscar Serlin's office in Rockefeller Center. Even the receptionist's room was quietly opulent. I gave the receptionist my name and she smiled and said: "Oh, yes!" and rang Mr. Serlin on the intercom, and then told me to go right in.

I opened the inner-office door and saw, across a vast expanse of carpeting, an imposing desk at the far end of the room from behind which a man rose and held out his hand. Oscar Serlin was over six feet tall and built like a football player. He gave me a warm handclasp, drew up a chair for me, offered me a cigarette from a silver box, lit it for me with a silver lighter, fixed his liquid brown eyes on me and said:

"Tell me about yourself,"

and as far as I was concerned, he was Shakespeare, Sir Galahad and President Roosevelt fused.

I gave him my ten-cent autobiography and he nodded. Then he

picked up the blue-bound copy of my play, which was on his desk.

"This is a very bad play," he said conversationally. "Your construction's lousy. Your two central characters are very interesting and your dialogue is excellent. But you have to be a carpenter before you can be a cabinet-maker. Let me show you."

And leaning back in his chair, he reconstructed the entire play for me so easily and brilliantly it left me tongue-tied. When I could speak, I told him I knew I could rewrite it exactly as he'd outlined it and that I thought I could finish it within the standard three-month option period.

It was then that he explained — with some surprise, I thought — that he didn't want to produce the play. He'd just wanted to meet me.

"I want you to keep in touch with me," he said, "and I want to see your next play. When are you moving back to New York?"

"I'm trying to find a job in Philly so I can earn enough to come back," I said, "but I haven't had any luck so far."

He nodded and wished me well and walked me to the door; and sadly relinquishing the dream of having my play produced by this god, I left his office and went over to the Taft Hotel to change into my new blouse in their ladies' room.

The Taft Hotel ladies' room charged me a nickel for the use of their john, which is the one health service I thought nobody ought to have to pay for, and I left there vowing never to patronize the Taft Hotel again.

Charlie lived way up on Riverside Drive. I caught a Fifth Avenue double-decker bus, climbed to the top and took the front seat so none of the other passengers could watch me counting my remaining funds. I had a return ticket, thirty-five cents and six cigarettes. Deduct a dime for a bus to Penn Station and another for a bus home from North Philadelphia station, and I had fifteen cents left over — exactly the price of a fresh pack of cigarettes for tomorrow — so I decided to make the six cigarettes last me till I got home to Philadelphia.

Charlie turned out to be a pleasant, bustling little man who welcomed me with enthusiasm and presented me proudly to the assembled dinner guests. They included an elderly lady backer who was deaf and had to be shouted at; a German baron who wrote poetry and planned to direct my play for Charlie though he'd never directed a play before; and a pair of homosexual male twins who were dying to act in my play, which had no parts for them. But everybody was enthusiastic about the play, the martinis were excellent — and all over the living room, on every table, were wooden boxes and crystal holders chockful of free cigarettes.

We drank to the play, we discussed possible stars for it, we debated whether the Booth Theatre was too small or the Belasco too big, and by the time Charlie led the way into the dining room I was carelessly dismissing Oscar Serlin as shortsighted.

All I remember about that dinner is my traumatic experience with the first course. Did I tell you I'm very nearsighted? Well, in those days, as Dorothy Parker observed, men never made passes at girls who wore glasses. Being young and female, I never wore mine at a dinner party, certainly not at a dinner party given in my honor by a Broadway producer. The first course arrived in the kind of sherbet glasses my mother used for shrimp cocktail, and all I could see of the stuff in the glass in front of me was that it was white. Peering narrowly down at it, I decided it was crab meat, of which I am very fond, and I took a hungry mouthful of it — and discovered, with apoplectic results, that it wasn't crab meat. I didn't know what it was, but I knew I couldn't swallow it. So, before the fascinated gaze of the entire dinner party, I spit it out.

"It's herring," Charlie told me. "Don't you like it?" — a question I bitterly resented since it would be rude to say no and having just spit it out I could hardly say yes. So I can't tell you what else we ate or what we talked about; I spent the rest of the dinner hour patching together the remnants of my aplomb.

After dinner, the other guests departed and Charlie took me to see his current Broadway play. The production was the kind usually described as "shabby": the sets didn't quite work, the direction was awkward and the play was embarrassing where it was meant to be moving. After the theatre, we adjourned to Sardi's — to talk.

At Sardi's, it turned out that while my play was still marvelous, it wasn't quite marvelous enough. It would be, however, as soon as Charlie rewrote it. What he had in mind was a contract making him co-author. He would then rewrite the play his way and if his version was approved by his backers, he'd produce it.

Had Oscar Serlin offered me such a contract I'd have jumped at it (though Oscar would have found the suggestion that he rewrite an author's play simply bizarre). But where Oscar's revised construction of the play had sounded brilliantly right, Charlie's sounded terrible. Nor did he bolster my confidence in him by telling me what changes he'd personally made in his current play. The scenes I'd found embarrassing were the scenes Charlie had written.

I explained this to Charlie. (Every year I make a vow to learn tact or keep my mouth shut but so far nothing has come of it.) We argued and we talked and we argued and we arrived at no conclusion. Sardi's, on the other hand, did: I looked up and noticed that the waiters were putting chairs up on tables and that we were the only customers left in the restaurant. I plucked Charlie's sleeve as he was finishing a sentence.

"I think Sardi's wants to close," I said.

We looked at Charlie's watch; it was nearly 3 A.M.

With many apologies, Charlie put me in a cab, gave the driver a dollar and said:

"Take the young lady to her hotel."

The cab drove off and I told the driver to take me to Penn Station. At Penn Station, the lone night clerk informed me that the next train for Philadelphia was due at 6:35. I couldn't wake up Maxine's family at three in the morning to ask to sleep there. So I sat down on a Penn Station bench to wait for the 6:35.

It was a raw March night, there wasn't anybody else in the waiting room, and Penn Station was saving heat. I'd been sitting there for fifteen chilly minutes trying to get up the nerve to ask the night clerk if he had a blanket, when the stationmaster came along. He stopped, looked down at me and asked politely what I was doing there.

"I'm waiting for the six-thirty-five to Philadelphia," I said.

He clucked.

"A nice young lady," he said, "doesn't want to sit all night in a railroad station!"

And I thought: You won't get any argument out of me, mister, there's no place I wouldn't rather sit.

"Wouldn't it be much better," he said, "to go across the street to the Governor Clinton Hotel and get a good night's sleep?"

I don't know why I couldn't tell him I only had thirty-five cents, but I couldn't. And since I was wearing my good suit and silk blouse he couldn't guess it.

"How will it be," he suggested jovially, "if I escort you there myself?" And he bowed and offered his arm.

I stood up and he took my arm and we left the station and walked across the street to the Governor Clinton, where the stationmaster explained to the desk clerk that this charming young lady had missed her train and needed a room for the night.

And don't think he didn't stand there at my side till the desk clerk gave me a little cellophane bag with a nightgown and toothbrush in it and summoned a bellhop to take me up to my room.

The bellhop took me up and unlocked the door and switched on the lights for me, and I tipped him a quarter — leaving me a total capital of ten cents, minus the cost of the room (and the nightgown and the toothbrush), which I hadn't had the courage to ask about.

I undressed, decided it was a lovely hotel, crawled into bed at quarter to four and slept like a baby till eleven-fifteen next morning.

At eleven-sixteen I phoned Maxine. It was Saturday and I prayed her rehearsal wasn't scheduled till noon, which was usual on a Saturday. God heard me and Maxine herself answered the phone.

"You have to come down and get me out of here," I said. "I'm at the Governor Clinton in a room I can't pay for. I don't even know how much it costs."

"Hang up, the operator may be listening in," said Maxine. "I'll be right down."

And she came down and paid the hotel bill. Since her play had been in rehearsal for three weeks and was due to open the following Tuesday (and close the following Saturday), Maxine was in funds and bought me a lavish breakfast before we had another weepy farewell and I went back to Philadelphia.

My mother brushed aside the bad news about the play.

"You've got a job!" she said. "In the press department of *Life With Father*. It's on the second floor of the Walnut Street Theatre, you start Monday. A man just called an hour ago."

Oscar Serlin had given the press agent's assistant a paid vacation for the remaining six weeks of the play's run in Philadelphia — just to make room for me, so I could earn my way back to New York.

Oscar and Charlie were only the beginning. During my two months in the *Life With Father* press office, through the two summer months when I worked as prop girl at a summer theatre in Philadelphia and on through September when I finally moved back to New York, I was positively besieged by producers. If producers Nos. 1 and 2 had conformed to Flanagan's Law, the rest of them positively shouted it.

Producer No. 3 was elderly and semiretired but he'd had a legendary career in his day.

"Yours is the first play he's been interested in in five years," said my agent, impressed. "He wants to take you to lunch."

I met the legendary producer for lunch at the Algonquin, where for two hours he talked of his producing days, the great stars and playwrights he'd discovered and the contrasting sorry state of the contemporary theatre. When we parted, he wished me every success and certainly hoped one of these younger fellows would have the sense to produce my play. (Agent's translation: "I guess he's broke.")

Producer No. 4 telephoned me at midnight. I'd never heard of him but what did that matter?

"I've just read your play and I'm so excited I can't sleep!" he said. "Can you lunch with me tomorrow?"

We lunched. He was an attractive young man and I gathered he had a private income. I asked what plays he'd produced.

"None yet," he said. "I've been looking for the right play for five years. Thanks to you, I've finally found it!"

He took a three-month option on the play. He wanted revisions, and during the next three months while I was rewriting, we met weekly to discuss the revisions over long and expensive lunches. At the end of three months, he read another playwright's play and realized that *that* was the one he'd spent five years looking for, and he dropped his option on mine and took an option on the new one. Three months later still, he dropped the second play, having found a third to take an option on and have long, expensive lunches over.

This man was what might be called a pretend-producer. There were quite a few of these. There was one man who sat in the same office for sixteen years reading plays. He never produced one. If you dropped in at his office, at your agent's suggestion, he told you he just hadn't been able to find the exactly right play. But he was still looking — and as a matter of fact, he had one play in

mind, a French play, and if the author was willing to rewrite —
and if the American rights were available — and if he could find
the right adapter for it, which was going to be tough because it
was a very special script, but as he'd told your agent, as soon as he
got a decent translation he wanted you to read it because you just
might be the right adapter for it, he wasn't sure. . . .

Producer No. 5 sent for me and when I walked into his office he
said: "How-d'ya-do" impatiently, and then before I even found a
chair: "The whole thing goes haywire in the second act, you're
going to have to do the whole play over. Sit down, I'll show you
what I want you to do." This one meant business.

He told me how he wanted the play rewritten. He was going to
Hollywood for two months and he wanted the revised play ready
for production when he came back. He asked whether I'd be
willing to quit my job and live on the option money, which he
would mail to my agent, so that I could work on the play full
time. I said yes.

I was working as secretary to a press agent and I quit the job
and went to work on the revisions. The producer sent me a long,
encouraging letter from Hollywood but he forgot to send my
agent the option money. The night before he was due back in
New York, I sat up till 4 A.M. to finish typing the revised draft and
put it between covers. At noon the next day I went to his office
with the finished play.

His secretary took my name in. Then she came back. The producer, she said, was about to go into rehearsal with a new play
and wouldn't have time to read mine. But he sent me greetings
and wished me lots of luck with the play. (None of us was so
sordid as to mention the unpaid option money.)

Producer No. 6 was a very fine actor who wrote me from Hollywood that he wanted to produce the play and star in it as soon as
he completed the film he was making. And he very well might
have done so if, three weeks after he wrote to me, he hadn't
happened to drop dead on the golf course of a heart attack.

And that was the end of the furor over that particular play.

Since this history was to be repeated, with minor variations, every time I hatched a play (and I had them like rabbits), I learned to understand how producers' minds worked.

When a producer phones a playwright and says: "You've written a wonderful play. When can you come and see me?" it doesn't mean he wants to produce the play. But whether it means (a) he wants to meet the playwright, or (b) he wants to rewrite the play himself to make it producible, or (c) he'd produce it if he had the money, or (d) he needs a play in reserve, to hold his backers' interest till he finds one he really likes, his motive stems from the same economic fact. That fact told me why the odds against me would always be so much greater than the odds against Maxine.

If you're a young actress who has never set foot on a professional stage, a producer can take a small gamble on you by giving you a bit part in his next production. If you do well, he'll trust you with a larger part next season. Eventually, he may trust you with a leading role.

But if you're a young playwright, the situation is different. There's no such thing as a bit play. It's going to cost a Broadway producer just as much to produce your play as to produce Tennessee Williams's. He can't take a small gamble on you; he's got to gamble all the way.

He reads your play and it's clearly not worth gambling the fortune required to produce a play on Broadway. But there's a fine central character and the last scene in the second act is terrific — and what about your next play? So he wants to meet you. And he definitely wants to see your next play.

He gets your next play a year later and it's not very good but it's better than the first one. And what about next year? Maybe your great play is just around the corner, maybe you just need to be nursed a little longer. So instead of returning the script to your agent with a flat rejection, the producer phones you.

"I've read your play and I'm very impressed," he says, which is true as far as it goes. "When can you lunch with me?"

And you lunch with him. For the first five years. After that, you don't bother unless you need the lunch because you know from experience, if they take you to lunch they don't want your play.

·4·

If She Takes You to Lunch
She Can't Sell It

A COUPLE OF TIMES in the last chapter I mentioned my agent without telling you who she was. The truth is I couldn't remember who she was. (I say "she" because in the forties and fifties, as almost all producers were men, almost all agents were women.)

"Agents" in this book, of course, refers exclusively to Broadway play agents — "playbrokers," they were once called. Those I knew were affectionate, warm-hearted women who belonged body and soul to their clients — unlike many Hollywood agents and New York literary agents who were rumored to be Uncle Toms (ostensibly working for their writers but actually far more zealous in looking after the interests of the Hollywood studio or the New York publishing house). But though I have fond memories of every playbroker who ever handled my plays, I managed to use up seven of them (that I can remember), some of them twice.

Beginning in my fellowship year, when the older playwrights in the seminar were already complaining about their agents, I noted a fact that became increasingly evident as the years went on. Since all (but one) of the unsuccessful playwrights I ever knew were men, I hope they'll excuse me for stating this fact in the male gender:

The average unsuccessful playwright goes through life with the firm conviction that his agent is persecuting him. She's giving him ulcers and sinus trouble and he complains about her to his friends and to the psychoanalyst she drives him to.

I couldn't afford ulcers or an analyst, so on the night when I discovered my agent was giving me a severe postnasal drip, I realized the time had come to figure out how agents' minds worked. Having run through three of them by then, I made a discovery which from then on was my salvation:

All playbrokers are alike.

Herewith the biography of a play agent, or what you need to know before you set foot in her office with your new play.

She begins her career by renting a small office and installing a phone, on capital saved while she was assistant to an older agent. She has pirated away two or three of the older agent's youngest clients, and she scouts around and corrals a few more potential playwrights, say eight in all. Her real assets are in herself: she is friendly and sympathetic, she is brilliantly critical, highly intelligent, shrewd and slightly ruthless.

She goes to work to sell her eight plays, sending each play to Broadway producers, and phoning and pestering selected stars and directors until they, too, agree to read her plays. As fast as a play comes back rejected, she sends it out again. And then one day, she sells one of the eight plays. It opens, it's a hit, and overnight the author is a big name on Broadway.

The agent now has Mr. Big to pay her office rent and phone bill. She has seven unsold plays, which six Broadway producers have read and rejected, and a dozen producers have not yet seen. They never will see those seven plays. Because now that the agent has Mr. Big, eight new clients drift in, wanting her to handle their plays. She's Mr. Big's agent: if she's good enough for him, she's good enough for them. So the agent gets to work on the eight new plays, and puts the seven old ones on a closet shelf marked *Dead.*

Well, why doesn't she try to sell all fifteen? Because she hasn't time. Why not? It doesn't take her all day to send out the new plays, does it? No — but she has Mr. Big.

Now that his play is a hit, she's busy negotiating a screen sale, she's attending rehearsals of the road company and sitting in on auditions for the London company — because having a big-name client means that the agent's not just an agent any more: she's Mr. Big's business manager, press representative, legal adviser, play doctor, confidante and best friend. She's his buffer in every argument he has with his producer, his director or his star, no matter how many arguments there are or how far into the night they run. If he has a second play trying out in Boston, she has to fly up for the opening: he needs her. If his New York hit opens in London, she has to fly over. Her time is not her own, her soul is not her own, they both belong to Mr. Big. And why not? He's paying the rent, the phone bill, the secretary's salary.

She therefore puts the old plays on the *Dead* shelf and goes to work to sell the new. She sells one. It opens and flops, but she unloads it on Hollywood for a small fortune. The author of this one isn't a big name, but he's made her some money, she has faith in his future and he needs help on his new play, the second act's giving him trouble. Meanwhile, of course, several of *his* friends bring her *their* plays because she's *his* agent: she got him all that Hollywood money and if she's good enough for him she's good enough for them.

So the agent puts the second batch of unsold plays on the *Dead* shelf and goes to work to sell the third. By which time, of course, the original seven unsold plays are so far down on the *Dead* shelf she's forgotten about them.

The authors of them, unfortunately, haven't.

The author of one of them, not having heard from his agent in several months, phones her one day to find out what's happening with his script.

"Just-a-minute-I'll-see-if-she's-free," says the secretary who answers his call. This is followed by a three-minute pause, during which the agent debates whether to duck the playwright or take the bull by the horns. She decides to take it by the horns. She gets on the phone.

"HelLO!" she says in a warmly personal voice. "When can we lunch?"

They lunch. Over the Bloody Marys, the agent tells the author what the last producer who saw his play said about it — not realizing she told him this three months ago and is exposing the fact that she hasn't sent it anywhere since. Over the entree she tells him the latest theatre gossip ("He was drunk last night when he made his third-act entrance, it's not his fault, poor soul, the man is Sick, he is So Sick!"). Over coffee, she asks the playwright when he's going to write a new play, he's too talented to be so lazy!

Now any idiot should know by this time that the agent has given up on his play. Our hero, however, refuses to believe it without further proof. In search of which, he strides briskly into her office one day between 1 and 3 P.M., when he knows she's out to lunch. (Agents transact much of their business over lunch so lunch invariably takes two hours.)

"I'd like to pick up a copy of my play," he says. "Olivier wants to read it."

He tells the secretary the title of his play and she looks puzzled: she's only worked here four months and she's never heard of that play.

"I'll see if I can find it," she says, and moves innocently, unerringly, toward the closet shelf marked *Dead*. The playwright, hard on her heels, stares over her shoulder and sees, in shocked outrage, all six copies of his play, all very dusty. The truth is there and he faces it squarely: this friendly, sympathetic, brilliantly critical, highly intelligent, shrewd and slightly ruthless woman hasn't been sending his play around.

Six Broadway producers have seen it. Twelve or fifteen producers haven't, and as things now stand, won't. What can he do about it?

Well, he can go home and call up his friends and tell them all what a slob his agent is, and wind up with ulcers, a psychoanalyst and a persecution complex. But will that get his play read by all the Broadway producers who haven't seen it? No, it won't. Then what's the solution? How is he to get his script into the hands of all the producers who haven't yet read it? The answer lies in that basic fact about agents: *All playbrokers are alike.*

This being so, when you find all six copies of your script on your agent's *Dead* shelf, this is what you do:

You wander into her office, unannounced, late one afternoon when you know she's finished work for the day and has time to talk. She welcomes you warmly (they always do), if defensively (ditto), and tells you to come on into her private office and talk to her.

You tell her honestly that you're sorry your play wasn't good enough for her to sell. And you love her dearly but would she be terribly hurt if you took it to some less important agent, who might be willing to send it to off-off-Broadway and little-theatre groups, which you realize she herself hasn't time to do.

Up to now, the agent's been feeling guilty about you, since along with her other virtues and contrary to general opinion she also has a conscience. And here you are, offering to take one guilt source off her mind. She's so grateful she smiles at you almost with tears in her eyes.

If she couldn't sell your play, she says, she hopes you know it wasn't for lack of trying, or lack of faith in you or affection for you. And what's more, she means it; and what's still more, realistically speaking it's true. So you tell her, with tears in *your* eyes, that you never doubted that. You and she part company with mutual affection and esteem. But — if by some chance you don't know their names by heart — before you leave, you ask her to give you a list of the six producers who rejected the play.

Armed with your list, and your six scripts, you proceed to the office of another agent and ask if she'll read your play. She has a Mr. Big too, of course, but he's in Hollywood at the moment so she has a little free time. She reads your play, she thinks it's salable and she offers to send it around. In her stable, you're a brand-new dark horse. She sends the play to the six best producers who haven't seen it. (Two of the six want to meet you, one takes you to lunch, and the other three reject it without all the ceremony.) Three months go by and you phone the agent to ask what's doing with the play. And she says:

"HelLO! When can we lunch?"

And a week after that, you have a frank heart-to-heart talk, you part with mutual affection and esteem, and you are off, with your list of producers who have rejected the play, to agent No. 3. By the time the third agent is through with it, every producer on Broadway has read it and rejected it and you can forget it. But you've probably written a new play by then.

Now it's true, as Maxine once observed, that if you follow my system for five or six years you'll have "run through every agent on Broadway like a dose of salts." But by the time this happens, three former assistants to three of your former agents have set up shop for themselves and are looking for their first batch of clients. So you go to each in turn.

And then? Why then, you just go back to the beginning and start over. You carry your new play into the office of good old agent No. 1.

She's delighted to see you again. You parted with mutual affection and esteem; your old play showed promise; for all she knows, your new one may be the hit of the season. And if she can't sell it, you won't make her feel guilty; you didn't last time. So she welcomes you with the enthusiasm reserved for new clients and sends your script to the six best producers who haven't yet seen it.

Only the second time round, when you telephone to ask what's doing, and she says:

"HelLO! When can we lunch?"

you say:

"Oh, honey, can I have a raincheck? I'm working like a dog on a new first act —"

because by this time, you know damn well if she takes you to lunch she can't sell it.

· 5 ·

The Underfoot
Free Enterprise System

SINCE KIDS TRYING TO CRASH the theatre require expensive instruction (which includes seeing the best plays and films) as well as expensive clothes in which to be Seen on occasion, and since they never have any money, they have to master the delicate, illegal art of getting everything for nothing. In the cultivation of this art, my friend Maxine had no equal.

Maxine and I saw every Broadway show and neighborhood movie free. I went to producers' lunches attired in Saks's best, Maxine took vocal lessons and I was tutored privately in Latin and Greek, and none of it cost us a dime. All I can remember us paying for were the ballet lessons we took from the Greek gentleman. Thanks to Maxine's negotiations, we paid him a dollar a week in a class where everybody else was paying two dollars.

What specially equipped Maxine for this art, besides an unflagging imagination and the nerve of Napoleon, was her unique ignorance of finance. I couldn't add or subtract too well, but Maxine's innocence in money matters was so total it amounted to a whole new theory of economics. I'll give you an example:

The autumn when I finally got back to New York after a six-month exile in Philadephia I had difficulty finding a job. My capital finally dwindling to $15, I told Maxine I couldn't meet the $10 weekly rent on my hotel room the next week unless I cut down to one meal a day. We were riding on the upper deck of a double-decker Fifth Avenue bus at the time, on our way up to Maxine's house for dinner, and Maxine stared thoughtfully out the window and down at the street as she worked on the problem.

"All right," she said finally. "The ten dollars a week for rent you can manage by putting a little away every day. Put fifty cents away every day; that way you won't miss it. And I can get the money for food for you. As long as I'm working part-time, you can collect my unemployment insurance; it's just sitting there!"

Given a mind like that, it's easy to evolve your own economic theory. Maxine's was simply stated:

Nothing should cost anything.

It went into operation that fall, when I finally got a job as assistant to a press agent. Salary: $25 a week. Ten dollars paid for the hotel room, three dollars went toward paying off a large dental bill, and the remaining twelve dollars were flung away carelessly on food, cigarettes, toothpaste, typing paper, typewriter ribbons, nylons, shoe repairs, carfare, semiannual haircuts and taxes. So by the time Friday — payday — came around, I was wiped out.

Since Maxine was living at home, her room, board and essential clothes were supplied. She was also working part-time taking street-corner surveys at one dollar per surveying hour. Surveys of corporation vice-presidents paid two dollars, but you didn't get this work often, and when you did, half the vice-presidents coldly refused to be surveyed; and since you got paid per vice-president instead of per hour, even that didn't pay too well. Her average weekly gross for four or five afternoons was twelve to fifteen dollars, which was distributed among hairdressers, theatrical makeup, street makeup, professional photos, Equity dues, audition accessories, nylons, cigarettes, carfare, agents' commissions, taxes and a monthly lunch at Sardi's. (If-you're-an-actress-you-have-to-be-Seen.) So as a rule, she had even less cash than I did.

I was therefore mildly startled when, shortly after I got the job,

Maxine phoned me at the office on a Wednesday morning and inquired casually:

"Do you feel like seeing the new Odets tonight?"

I said I had $1.85 to last me till Friday if that answered her question.

"I don't mean buy tickets!" said Maxine impatiently. "Where would I get the money to buy tickets? I mean Just Go."

I had no idea what Just Go meant but I said I'd love to.

"Meet me at the drugstore on the corner of Forty-fifth Street at quarter to nine," she said. "Don't wear a coat."

It was a chilly November evening and the curtain time for Clifford Odets's play was eight-thirty, but I did as I was told. Maxine met me at the door of the drugstore and said briskly:

"We're all set. I phoned the box ofice and they're not sold out; they have a few seats downstairs."

We climbed on stools and ordered coffee and Maxine explained the Just Go method of seeing every show in town. We made our coffee last twenty minutes, during which we took turns running to the front door, at two-minute intervals, to glance up the street at the theatre where the Odets was playing. At nine-ten, it was my turn to be lookout and I saw the theatre doors open and the crowd begin to stream out onto the sidewalk for intermission.

We left the drugstore and hurried up the street to the theatre, to light cigarettes and mingle with the crowd of smokers on the sidewalk. After a few minutes, we drifted into the lobby and mingled with the smokers there. And when the bell rang, we mingled into the theatre along with the paying customers who went down the aisle to their seats. We stood at the back while Maxine, under pretext of wanting a last puff on her cigarette, cased the house for empty seats. These were easy to spot because they had no coats or programs on them. Maxine saw a pair down front on the side and said: "Come on."

She sailed down the aisle, her burnished head arrogantly high above her best black cocktail dress, her mother's marten scarf dangling negligently over one shoulder, and me pattering nervously behind her. She said, "Excuse me" graciously to a man sitting in the aisle seat and we climbed past him and sat down in the two empty seats. Maxine shook out her fur, draped it over the back of her chair and turned to survey the house.

"There are two better seats back there in the center," she said, and stood up. "Come on."

"You go if you want to," I said. I was pale with terror.

"Is this really your first time?" she asked sympathetically. I nodded and she sat back down.

"All right," she said. "We forgot to get programs. After the second act, remind me."

The house lights dimmed and I sat frozen in the certainty that at any second an usher's hand would drop to my shoulder and a waiting cop would haul Maxine and me off to night court. But no usher materialized: we saw the second act of the Odets, which was excellent; and after the second intermission we picked up a pair of programs and moved to the better seats on the center aisle.

From then on, we went to theatre several nights a week. We never saw a first act, but in a three-act play nothing ever happened in the first act. Of course, it wasn't always smooth sailing. Occasionally the house proved to be more crowded than the box office had indicated when we phoned; and as the houselights dimmed, we'd find ourselves still standing at the back or, worse still, wandering up and down the aisle looking for empty seats — at which moment an usher was likely to loom up and helpfully ask to see our stubs.

"I'm afraid we've lost them," Maxine would explain in her best stage diction. "We must have dropped them in the lobby during intermission." And we'd flee out to the lobby and across the street, and wait around to mingle with the intermission crowd at the musical there. (Musicals were in two acts instead of three and had a single later intermission.)

Since the biggest hits somehow always opened in the winter

months, we caught a lot of colds. You can't mingle into a theatre with an intermission crowd in your winter coat. The ushers would spot you at once as a gate-crasher, since no matter what the weather theatregoers always leave their coats behind on their seats when they go out for a smoke. So on cold nights, Maxine caught sore throats walking to her subway and I got coughs standing on windy corners waiting for my bus. But if you go to theatre regularly, it ought to cost you *something*. Especially if the show was a rare and wonderful one like *Lady in the Dark*.

Lady in the Dark was the only musical ever to win the hearts of us two serious students of the drama. It had Gertie Lawrence, who had been our idol in half a dozen Broadway comedies, and it had an astonishing new comedian named Danny Kaye. We must have mingled into it half a dozen times and I remember the night when we made a momentous decision and spent our own money to see the first act. And still, when the show finally closed, our appetite for it was unappeased.

Soon after it closed, it went on the road and opened in Philadelphia. Philadelphia being my home town, I considered it squarely up to me to get us there. My father knew the box-office men, so getting in to see the show free would be no problem. The problem was the fare to Philly. Neither of us had it.

On the Monday *Lady in the Dark* was to open in Philly, I brooded over the problem during breakfast at the cafeteria. Then I opened *The Times* and turned to the theatre section. In the middle of one page, an ad announced that tomorrow evening, the Philadelphia Orchestra would give its regular Tuesday concert at Carnegie Hall. Right there, the problem was solved.

On my way from the cafeteria to the office, I worked out a story to give my boss about having to go to Philadelphia Wednesday for a funeral. Then I phoned Maxine.

"Meet me at Carnegie Hall at eight-thirty tomorrow night," I said. "Bring a nightgown. Tell your folks you'll be back Wednesday night late."

I had in my adolescence been one of several thousand bobby-sox worshippers of Leopold Stokowski, conductor of the Philadelphia Orchestra. With all my friends I had got happily in the orchestra's hair, I knew all the first-desk men personally and was especially palsy with Marshall Betz, the orchestra librarian.

Therefore when Maxine met me at Carnegie Hall, we went around to the stage door and said hello to Marshall, who passed us in to hear the concert. During intermission we went backstage to say hello to my many friends in the orchestra and put through a call to my father on the Carnegie Hall office phone asking him to meet us at Broad Street Station at approximately one in the morning. We heard the rest of the concert and then rode to Philadelphia on the Philadelphia Orchestra's private train.

I had one bad moment on the train when Maxine, looking extremely high-fashion in a dark green wool suit and her mother's fur jacket, turned to me and said simply:

"Stick close to me, will you? I only have a nickel."

My father drove us home and we slept in the twin beds in my old bedroom. *Lady in the Dark* was sold out, of course. But we got passed in to hang over the back rail at the matinee performance, dined with my parents, hung over the back rail again for the evening performance and touched my father for the fare back to New York. He also drove us to the station so that when we reached New York, Maxine still had her nickel. It took her home on the subway.

We had an easier time seeing neighborhood movies free. We only had to miss the credits, and the M-G-M lion or J. Arthur Rank's naked friend banging his gong. Maxine and I were selective moviegoers: we only saw half a dozen films a year, but we saw each of them five or six times. We'd get a crush on James Mason, say, or Humphrey Bogart, and follow his current film from the upper West Side to lower Third Avenue. We saw *The Maltese Falcon* seven times and *I Know Where I'm Going* six. With *The*

Seventh Veil, I lost count. This kind of moviegoing was ideally suited to Maxine's system, which ruled out patronizing any one movie theatre often enough for the box-office girl to get to know our faces.

What we did was, we phoned the box office and asked when the last feature started. If the box office said eleven o'clock, we'd get to the movie house at eleven-ten, and lurk outside a few minutes till the box-office girl closed up and went home. Then we just walked in and sat down. Any usher not in the men's room changing into his street clothes was asleep in the back row.

Only once did we have to wait outside an extra ten minutes till the manager came out and went home. This was at a movie theatre where, on a previous nerve-racking evening, we had unexpectedly bumped into him coming out as we were going in.

You may have noticed I was careful to specify neighborhood movie houses. Only once did we attempt a first-run Broadway house. The Broadway movie palaces were great, plush Hollywood temples crawling with doormen and uniformed ticket takers and different grades of ushers, and you couldn't possibly sneak in free, even at midnight. It was this impasse that led Maxine and me to commit our only prison offense.

I was working late that evening at the press office, folding, inserting, sealing and stamping five hundred press releases which had to be mailed that night to newspapers all over the country on behalf of a second-rate tenor who was going on a cross-country tour. I was dining on a sandwich and a container of coffee and folding the last hundred letters when Maxine wandered in. She'd had a late rehearsal at a theatre across the street and had seen the light in the press office window.

"The new Bogart opened today at the Capitol," she remarked.

The Capitol being a very overstaffed palace, I told her plainly I only had ninety cents. She only had ten. As tickets were $1.25 per person, I considered the subject closed. I went on folding and

Maxine sat down and inserted the letters for me and we sealed and stamped them. As I put away the leftover releases and envelopes and the leftover sheets of stamps, Maxine rose.

"I think I'll phone the Capitol," she said.

She found the number and dialed it. I took a last mouthful of coffee and then nearly choked to death on it as I heard Maxine's most gracious stage voice inquire of the Capitol box office:

"Do you accept stamps?"

There was a brief pause, and then Maxine amplified:

"Postage stamps. In exchange for tickets."

She listened a minute, said, "Thank you" warmly and hung up.

"They'll take them," she said. "Where did you put them?"

"It's stealing!" I said.

"On what you're paid?" said Maxine coldly. "You were supposed to leave an hour ago. Are you being paid for overtime?"

So a few minutes later we pushed two dollars and fifty cents' worth of stamps across the counter at the box office of the Capitol Theatre and went to see Humphrey Bogart in *Casablanca*.

While free entertainment was something we both required, free clothes were needed only by me, since Maxine's parents were still happy to keep her supplied with Bendel's best. My clothes problem was chronic but I was blessed with affluent friends who were always generously deciding they never wore that old plaid suit anymore, or With skirts getting longer that raincoat was really much too short. And if a skirt was too large at the waist or a dress, in Maxine's phrase, "hung like a bag" on me, I'd early resigned myself to the fact that I couldn't sew and couldn't afford alterations and I went around unconcernedly pinned together. So whenever Maxine and I were strolling on Fifth Avenue and she wanted to stop in at Bergdorf's or Bendel's, she'd pause on the sidewalk in front of the store, run an eye over my conglomerate outfit and say simply:

"You wait out here."

But of course there were critical producers' lunches and large romantic evenings for which I had to look the part. On most of these occasions I just borrowed Maxine's clothes, having had the forethought to get thin enough to wear them. But every now and then, both of us had important engagements for the same day or evening and Maxine would report with distress that she didn't have two suitably elegant ensembles on hand.

In such emergencies I followed her instructions. I went to Saks, bought a beautiful dress or suit on my charge account, took it home, wore it on my big date, and returned it to Saks the next day. (Except that, being sloppy, I generally got a spot on it, in which case I kept it and paid it off at the rate of five dollars a month for a year or two so that by the time I threw it out it was all paid for.)

Maxine borrowed my clothes only once. She borrowed a ruffled organdy blouse handed down to me by some sadist, my five-year-old black suit and a beanie my mother had knitted, which was my hat wardrobe that season.

"What do you want them for?" I demanded. Maxine looked evasive.

"I'll take care of them," she said.

Two weeks later, when she returned them, I found out she'd worn them on location in a rooming house in Brooklyn, where she'd played the lead in a documentary film on gonorrhea.

When it came to vocal lessons for Maxine, and Latin and Greek lessons for me, we hit our first snag. I'd been trying to teach myself Latin and Greek and she'd been trying to teach herself to carry a tune and neither of us was doing too well.

Private instruction being both necessary and expensive, Maxine decided that the solution for both of us was to Sell Something. This led to two exhausting Saturdays, the first spent haggling with the Empire Diamond and Gold Buying Service over the value of my high school graduation ring and a ring my parents had given me with a minute diamond in it, for both of which Empire gave me a stingy fifteen dollars, and since this wouldn't buy much Greek I bought Shaw and Shakespeare with it instead.

The second Saturday we spent trotting from secondhand clothing store to secondhand clothing store trying to sell Maxine's mother's fifteen-year-old Persian lamb coat. That coat gave Maxine nothing but trouble anyway. Her mother had passed it on to her a couple of years before, and for a whole season Maxine had worn it with chic assurance. But during the second season, she made the mistake of wearing it on a picket line she had volunteered for. You turn up on a line of starving strikers wearing a Persian lamb coat and you are liable to be stoned to death. Maxine escaped without injury but she lost her taste for the coat, so one hot Saturday in August we lugged it to the Ritz Thrift Shop ready to trade it in for vocal lessons.

"How much are you asking?" said the man at the Ritz Thrift Shop, running a practiced eye over the coat.

"I thought two hundred," said Maxine in a tone that managed to be both haughty and friendly.

"Oh, we can't even talk!" said the man. When pressed, he allowed the coat might be worth forty dollars to him. Outraged, we stalked out of there and lugged the coat in and out of all the secondhand stores on Sixth Avenue and Eighth Avenue and then we went across town and lugged it down Second Avenue and up Third, and at five o'clock we gave up and lugged it back to the Ritz Thrift Shop and Maxine took the forty dollars, which paid for eight vocal lessons.

The problem of my Greek and Latin lessons remained unsolved. I wrote dignified letters to all the free city colleges, none of which, it turned out, gave free night courses in Latin and Greek. I took my one remaining piece of jewelry — a lapel watch — down to the Empire Diamond and Gold Buying Service and they wouldn't even make me an offer. Just as I was getting completely discouraged, Maxine, as usual, came through with the solution.

"Why don't you run an ad in the Personals column of the *Saturday Review?*" she suggested.

"The problem isn't finding a tutor," I said. "It's finding the money to pay him!"

"That's all right," said Maxine reasonably. "Just mention in the ad that you can't pay anything."

And if you think I got no response to an ad that read:

> Wish to study Latin and Greek.
> Can't pay anything.

you underestimate the readers of the *Saturday Review*. I got five offers, one from a German refugee who said he would teach me the Latin and the Greek if I would teach him the English, two from retired professors, and one from a Lebanese rug merchant who didn't know Latin but offered to teach me modern Greek and Arabic instead.

The fifth letter came from a young man who wrote that he'd graduated from the Roxbury Latin School and Harvard; and after careful consideration, Maxine advised me to award the coveted post to him.

"In the first place, he's young and he might be cute," she pointed out. "And in the second place, you can't do better than Harvard."

So Tom Goethals, who turned out to be six-feet-four, lean and shy-looking, and whose grandfather had built the Goethals Bridge, put his Roxbury Latin School and Harvard education to use by teaching me to read Catullus and trying to teach me Greek grammar.

Maxine phoned me after the first lesson.

"How was he?" she asked.

"Oh, he's great!" I said.

"I told you to stick to Harvard," she said. "Taking somebody second-rate would be like sneaking into theatre and sitting in the balcony, or borrowing clothes from Gimbel's instead of Saks. If you're getting things for nothing, it's just as easy to get the best."

We always got the best.

·6·

"Sumer Is Icumen In..."

"I HAVE TO STAY HOME tonight," I told Maxine on the phone one April evening when she wanted to go to theatre. "I have to write my summer-theatre letters."

"I'm set, thank God," said Maxine. She'd been hired for the summer as a member of the resident company trying out new plays at the Theatre Guild's summer playhouse in Westport, Connecticut.

The summer-theatre furor always began in April when the new *Summer Theatre Directory* appeared on the Times Square newsstand. The day it came out, you tore down to Times Square along with every other brat in show business, bought your copy and took it home, and spent the evening making a list of first-, second-, and third-choice barns to spend the summer in, as a member of the acting company, the backstage crew or the producer's staff.

Somehow, anyhow, you got yourself set for the summer, and in June you quit your winter job and set out for the Adirondacks or the coast of Maine where you had an absolutely wonderful two months on a schedule that would have put a normal person in a sanitarium and at a salary Charles Dickens would have refused to believe.

There were two kinds of summer theatres: the pre-Broadway tryout house, like the Guild's playhouse in Westport, and the "package" theatre, where each week a star arrived with an acting company (the "package") with which he or she was touring the summer circuit in some old war-horse like *Candida* or *Charley's Aunt.*

I didn't care which kind of theatre I worked in, and that night I wrote to a dozen summer-theatre producers offering myself as prop girl, scene painter, assistant stage manager or typist willing to double as usher. (The only category I omitted was box-office ticket seller. I can't add.) A few weeks later I landed a job and had myself a superb summer but it got off to a demoralizing start.

One of my letters had gone to a man who ran the Bucks County Playhouse in New Hope, Pennsylvania, not far from Philadelphia. He had phoned me, interviewed me and engaged me as his secretary for the summer. I was to report at Bucks on June 20.

On June 20, I arrived in New Hope and hauled my two suitcases into the playhouse office. The producer looked up from his desk and stared at me blankly.

"What can I do for you?" he asked. I told him he'd hired me as his secretary for the summer. "Oh!" he said. "That was last spring, wasn't it? I thought my secretary was going to be working for Bela Blau up at the Deertrees Theatre in Maine. I talked her into staying with me." I must have turned pale because he added: "Maybe they haven't replaced her yet. Why don't I phone and see if they can use you at Deertrees?"

He phoned Deertrees, chatted a minute, hung up and said:

"They can use you."

I was to go back to New York and report to Bela Blau's office. Two members of the Deertrees staff were driving up that afternoon and Bela would phone his office and tell them to wait for me.

First I took a bus to Philadelphia, having a filial urge to see my parents and borrow the fare to Maine in case something went wrong in New York. Then I took a train back to New York and lugged my suitcases into Bela Blau's office and met the Deertrees stage manager, Bill Flanagan of Flanagan's Law, and the assistant stage manager who drove us to Maine in his elderly cream-colored Ford called the Beige Bee because he'd bought it with money he'd earned on a radio show called The Green Hornet.

The town of Harrison, Maine, lay between two lakes with mountains rising beyond them and was as beautiful a spot as I've ever seen. It was a tiny town — pop. 200 — with three streets. We found the theatre just beyond the third street and it was as enchanting as its setting. The handsome log-cabin playhouse stood in the center of a hushed clearing circled by pine woods. As we walked around to the back of the theatre to Bela Blau's office, the ground under our feet was a thick carpet of pine needles.

Bela shook hands with me and said, beaming:

"Your partner will be very glad to see you! She's a local girl and she almost quit when she thought she was going to be in there by herself. She's never worked in a box office before."

I did not say "In a *where?*" and I did not tell him I couldn't add. If Bela Blau wanted me looking after his finances for the summer, that was his problem. Mine was to get myself installed in a summer theatre. After a day of considerable mental anguish I was finally installed in one and I wasn't leaving.

Still, as I crawled into bed that night, in an airy bedroom in an old-fashioned frame house that let rooms to "summer people," I couldn't help feeling Bela Blau was in for a nerve-racking summer. And boy, was I right.

I met Reta Shaw, my cell-mate, the next morning. Reta was a stout schoolteacher with a pretty face and the most cheerful, unruffled disposition I've ever had the privilege of working alongside. She must have caught Theatremanja in that box office because the next year she gave up teaching and went to New York to crash the theatre — and did. She began turning up on Broadway as a comedienne in *Gentlemen Prefer Blondes* and *Picnic* and *The Pajama Game* and so forth; she was very much in demand for years.

She couldn't add either.

The two of us were on duty in the box office from 9 A.M. to 9 P.M. daily including Sunday. Salary: $17 a week. Eight of it paid the rent on the furnished room with breakfast thrown in, a dollar went for cigarettes (thirteen cents a pack in Maine that summer) and the remaining eight dollars bought seven lunches and seven dinners. The town of Harrison had one restaurant: Ken's Koffee Kup. If you didn't feel like eating there you could always starve. I have fond memories of Ken's place. The *cuisine* may not have been very *haute* but you got a lot of food there for eight dollars a week.

Deertrees ran on the package system. In successive weeks, we had Tallulah Bankhead, Ethel Barrymore, Grace George, each with her touring company and her ancient hit. Grace George, who had been a reigning star when my father was a chorus boy, had long since grown old enough and rich enough to spend her summers sensibly in Europe. Instead, she was touring the summer circuit in *Kind Lady*.

She arrived with her company at nine o'clock of a rainy Sunday night, having spent the day on the road from New Jersey where she'd played the week before. She announced that she would run through the play then and there, so that she and her company could accustom themselves to the new stage before the Monday night opening. But as I said, it was raining. Grace George walked into the theatre and realized there was going to be a hitch in her plans.

Deertrees was built entirely of pine logs, by somebody who didn't realize that the sound of steady rain on pine walls and a pine roof is deafening. During a heavy downpour, the players' voices were completely drowned out and the show simply stopped. When the rain let up — ten minutes or two hours later — the show resumed. So at nine o'clock that Sunday night, Grace George and her company sat down in the damp playhouse to wait out the storm. The crew and staff drifted in and we all sat around, listening to the racket and batting at the bugs which had hurried in out of the wet. At ten, we began to wonder when Miss George would give up and go to bed.

At a little before eleven, the rain stopped. And Grace George went up onstage with her company, and instead of walking through the play as the old lady held prisoner by two strangers and their half-witted daughter, gave a harrowing, electrifying performance that froze us to our seats. The performance ended at 1:30 A.M., after which Grace George, seventy if she was a day, sashayed serenely off to bed, looking forward to eight performances in the next six days with another traveling Sunday at the end of the week and *that's* what I mean by Theatremania.

Her opening-night performance was fine, but no finer than the performance she'd given for the staff and crew at midnight the night before, so we toasted her at our regular opening-night gin picnic. Each week, every member of the staff and crew gave Flanagan thirty-five cents and he bought gin and pretzels with it, and after the opening we had a gin picnic on the playhouse lawn. One Monday night we drank two-hundred-proof hospital alcohol instead. One of the boys on the crew had a brother who was an intern at a local hospital and he filched us a bottle of hospital alcohol which we cut with Coca-Cola. You can get higher on that than you can get on Cutty Sark. You can get positively looping till after a while you can't feel your arms or legs or anything.

As I said, Maxine was spending the summer at a "tryout" playhouse. A letter from her described the daily Westport routine and at first glance it seemed to be the standard schedule for an acting company at any summer theatre where a new play was tried out every week.

9:30 A.M.	Breakfast.
10:00 A.M.	Everybody off to study his-or-her lines in next week's play.
11:30–4:30	Rehearsal of next week's play.

4:30–6:00	More studying of lines in next week's play.
6:00–7:00	A light supper.
7:15	Arrive in dressing room to mend and press costumes and apply makeup.
8:30–11:00 P.M.	On stage in this week's play.
11:30	Late supper and then home to bed at one in the morning, in order to be up at nine and start the whole thing over again.

Wednesdays and Saturdays the program changed to include a matinee performance, and Sunday was entirely different: dress parade in the morning, dress rehearsal all afternoon and evening and far into the night.

Perfectly normal summer schedule. But Maxine's letter had been written in somebody's car on the way to Mount Kisco, New York, thus revealing an extra feature of the Westport company's schedule.

At Mount Kisco, which was forty miles from Westport, there was a playhouse of the "package" kind; and that summer Westport and Mount Kisco traded plays. Every alternate week, Westport sent its new tryout play to Kisco for a week's run, and Kisco sent its star "package" to Westport for a week. The "package" company, of course, just moved to Westport for the week. But the Westport company had to be in Westport during the day to rehearse next week's play, so instead of moving to Kisco the company commuted nightly.

So every second week, the six o'clock supper was sandwiches eaten in the car on the forty-five-minute drive to Kisco, and the eleven-thirty supper was sandwiches eaten in the car on the way back. It made a nice change for everybody.

By comparison, Reta and I had an easy summer in the box office. We whiled away the long hours between customers by playing word games and paper-and-pencil games: Battleship and Hangman and Associations and Twenty Questions and What Is It? On non-matinee days each of us was allowed to take the box office alone for two afternoon hours while the other went swimming or rowing — or just stood outside and felt the sun and saw the sky, which all by itself was a change.

Those afternoons gave us the strength to face the trauma of matinee days. The trauma was due to a crisis which arose absolutely incessantly.

As regularly as Wednesday matinee time arrived, either (a) some camp descended on us, 200 campers and 15 counselors strong, demanding the tickets they'd sent us a check for — only we'd thought they were coming Saturday so we'd saved 215 Saturday seats and sold today's seats to 215 other customers, and since the theatre only seated 300, there was no place to put the camp; or (b) we had 215 seats saved for the camp and the camp never showed up, having meant their check to cover 215 seats for *next* Wednesday.

This crisis took a lot out of us every time, not to mention what it took out of Bela Blau. He was a very kind and good-humored man and he never once lost his temper with us, but after the first three or four matinee days he began to acquire a hunted look. By the end of July all the fight went out of him, and for the rest of the summer the three of us simply resigned ourselves to a succession of traumatic Wednesday and Saturday afternoons.

Saturday was frantic altogether. Ticket sale in the morning, then the matinee crisis, then the evening ticket-sale rush, and at nine o'clock, when we closed the box office to the public, we had the entire week's receipts to tot up and balance. Including subtracting the tax on each ticket. I suppose if you had any talent for math you could have totted up our week's gross in half an hour, but it took Reta Shaw and me from nine till midnight, even with Bela helping. And when we were all through we were usually a dollar short.

At midnight on Saturday, we went into the theatre for our voluntary job of keeping the backstage crew awake and on their toes all night as they struck last week's set and mounted next week's. Reta and I made coffee and played records for them till four or five in the morning while they hauled scenery under Flanagan's supervision.

I'll tell you how he happened to explain Flanagan's Law to me. It was on a horrendous night when the male star of the show arrived in his dressing room fifteen minutes before curtain time, roaring drunk. Flanagan came charging out to the box office to tell us the news and describe the uproar backstage. Since the play was a comedy, I said:

"He may get through it, drunk as he is. The audience may think he's just playing the part very broadly. Otherwise it'll be a fiasco and we'll have to return their money."

"Neither will happen," said Flanagan, "because you predicted them. If you can predict it, it doesn't happen. In the theatre, no matter what happens to you, it's unexpected."

So of course I bet him one or the other would happen.

Bela Blau held the curtain till nine, but the star was still too drunk to walk straight or talk distinctly, and it was impossible to keep the audience waiting longer. At nine, Reta and I closed the box office and hurried into the theatre and hung over the back rail and watched in suspense as the curtain rose and the two minor characters who opened the play began their ten-minute scene, at the end of which the star was to make his entrance.

Five minutes after the play began, there was a reverberating clap of thunder followed by a torrent of rain on the pine roof and walls and the play came to an abrupt halt. The curtain fell, the houselights went up and the audience settled good-naturedly to wait out the storm.

At a little after ten, the rain stopped — by which time the star had been dragged out into the rain and forced to swallow a vat of black coffee, and when the curtain rose again he was thoroughly sober.

The play proceeded without a hitch and I've believed in Flanagan's Law ever since.

·7·

"No Legs No Jokes No Chance"

It began in December of 1942, the morning after the opening of a Guild flop called *The Russian People*. Despite the fact that we'd waited up till 4 A.M. for the notices, Joe and I were at work at 10 A.M. as usual, composing ads that would fool the public into thinking the show was a hit. Joe was the Theatre Guild press agent. I was his assistant.

We'd only had four hours' sleep but we were both wide awake. You couldn't possibly get drowsy in the Theatre Guild press department, not in December. Our top-floor offices got whatever heat was left over from the casting department on the floor below, the executive offices on the floor below that, and the theatre itself, which was on the ground floor.

The Russian People was a ponderous bore about the Nazis and the Russian front. But Joe, like the good press agent he was, had persuaded himself by opening night that it was the greatest thing since *Hamlet* and he took the notices hard. So we weren't talking much that morning. We just glumly pulled quotes for the ads.

Pulling quotes worked like this. If Brooks Atkinson, the *Times* drama critic, wrote: "For the fourth time this season, the Theatre Guild has wasted a superb production on a dull and empty play," you pulled out the two good words and printed at the top of your ad:

"SUPERB PRODUCTION!" — Atkinson; *Times*.

This sort of thing takes practice, but by the time *The Russian People* opened, we'd had a lot of practice. Not to beat about the bush, *The Russian People* was the Guild's sixteenth straight flop. It was only the eighth for me; I'd only worked there a year and a half.

I'd got the job when I came back from Deertrees. My agent phoned me one day and said Miss Helburn had read my new play and wanted to see me and the next afternoon I went to Terry's office.

"Dear," she said, "I don't like this play much. But I wanted to find out how you're getting on."

I told her I was out of work and starving to death and Terry asked what jobs I'd had. When I mentioned Oscar Serlin's press department and the press agent I'd worked for the season before she nodded.

"Joe Heidt, our press agent, needs an assistant," she said. "He's on the fourth floor. Run up and tell him I said you need the job and you're very bright."

So I took the elevator up to the fourth-floor attic and went down the hall past the auditor's office to the press department. Lois, Joe's secretary, was sitting in the outer office, surrounded by the usual press-department litter of newspapers, posters, glossy photos of stars and albums of press clippings. I asked if I might see Mr. Heidt and she told me to go on into the inner office.

Joe was sitting with his feet up on the desk reading a newspaper. He had a round Irish face which peered at me above the newspaper inquiringly.

"Miss Helburn sent me up," I said. "She said you need an assistant."

I stopped, being too shy to sell myself, and waited for him to ask where I'd worked before and whether I knew how to interview stars and write publicity stories for newspapers. I didn't realize the weight of the simple "Miss Helburn sent me up."

"Well, all right," said Joe resignedly. "You want to put your typewriter over there?"

And he peered into the outer office and pointed to a spot near Lois's desk. Lois and I got the former assistant's typewriter from the floor of a closet and put it over there, and I was assistant to the Theatre Guild press agent.

Part of my job was to go to all Guild openings to help Joe with the Critics' Seating List. And at my first Theatre Guild opening it was heaven to be standing between Joe and Johnny, the casting director, all of us leaning our elbows on the broad, plush-covered railing behind the last row of seats as the last glittering couples in evening gowns and dinner jackets followed an usher down the center aisle.

Our eyes swept the packed rows of first-night celebrities, a sea of carefully groomed heads that rolled away to the stage. Then the houselights dimmed and went out and in the black theatre the footlights gleamed like a golden ribbon along the edge of the dark stage and as the curtain slowly rose I think I stopped breathing.

This heady excitement returned with each of the next three openings. Then it wore off. You couldn't possibly assist at the string of disasters the Guild produced that season and the next, and retain your starry-eyed enthusiasm for opening nights.

The first show I worked on was *Hope for a Harvest*, which flopped so badly that the stars, Fredric March and his wife, Florence Eldridge, took an ad in the newspapers the next day with a cartoon of a trapeze artist missing connections with his partner in midair and a caption reading, "Oops! Sorry!"

Subsequent accidents included *Papa Is All*, which was Pennsylvania Dutch; *Mr. Sycamore*, in which Stuart Erwin became a tree in the second act (that is not a misprint and you did not misread it); and *Yesterday's Magic*, in which Paul Muni, as an alcoholic actor, threw himself out the window in the last scene. Add a couple of ill-fated revivals of classics, a limp comedy called *Without Love*, which not even Katharine Hepburn had been able to prop up for long, and finally, on this morning in December, *The Russian People*.

Looming up ahead, according to the brochure we'd sent to Guild subscribers in nineteen subscription cities, was a new American Folk Opera. Like *Porgy and Bess*, we assured everybody. It was to be based on an old Guild flop, and in true operatic tradition it was to have a murder committed onstage and a bona fide operatic ballet.

Considering our track record on even the most standard fare, this projected opera had given everybody the jimjams. But it was to be the Guild's most expensive venture in years, and the rumor that reached us that morning put an end to our worries about the Folk Opera. The rumor was that after sixteen flops, the Guild was bankrupt. Word spread from floor to floor that Terry and Lawrence were planning to sell the Guild Theatre and the Guild building to pay their debts. When the sale was complete, the Theatre Guild would cease to exist.

People from the other departments wandered morosely up to our offices that day, to indulge in the usual morning-after castigation of the management. Our attic was ideal for this, since it was the one place in which Terry and Lawrence could be counted on not to set foot, especially in December. All day long, the wage slaves from casting, subscription, auditing, playreading came in to sing the usual litany freely and with feeling. This would not have happened (the litany began)

— if Terry didn't sit over at the hairdresser's letting some floozy pick her plays for her;

— if Lawrence didn't lie on the casting couch plucking lofty, expensive ideas out of that goddamn mustache, with a vast unconcern for what the public would pay to see;

— if, when the lofty ideas flopped, the two of them didn't embark on monster economy drives which consisted of cutting down the number of towels rented weekly for each office and threatening to take the water cooler out of the casting department because (said Lawrence) too many strangers were drinking our water;

— and if, year after year, they didn't insist on selling season tickets in nineteen subscription cities for "six forthcoming Guild productions" when they had only four plays under option and disagreed violently about three of them.

And so on and so forth. It was an old refrain with lots and lots of verses. But on this December day the tone was particularly bitter. Not just because December was a very cold month in which to be thrown out of work, but because for all their talk nobody who worked there was eager to see the Theatre Guild close down. Most of them had been there for years. They remembered the great days of the Lunts, the Shaw openings and the five-hour O'Neill drama which the stage doorman was said to have referred to innocently throughout its run as "Strange Intercourse."

Joe and I finished making up the ads, and then he went down to get Lawrence's O.K. on them, and I went down to get Terry's.

She was in her office in an armchair, having tea. Her fluffy white hair was rinsed a deep, cerulean blue that season; her blunt nose and blunt chin were as cheerfully pugnacious as ever.

"Well, dear!" she said when I came in. "We seem to be having a run of bad luck!"

I gave her the ads and she read them carefully, glancing at the reviews to check each quote, then running her eye over all the reviews and murmuring:

"I don't know what the boys want!"

Then she said the ads were fine and handed them back to me, and I started for the door. As I reached it she said, patting her hair casually:

"I notice Lawrence was first on the program again. That's twice in a row, isn't it?"

If the program for one show read "Produced by Lawrence Langner and Theresa Helburn," the program for the next show had to read "Produced by Theresa Helburn and Lawrence Langner."

I said I was sure Mr. Langner hadn't been first twice in a row because Joe was always careful to check the last program before we made up the new one.

"All right," she said agreeably. "Just remind Joe: I'm first on the new one."

My gloom evaporated. *The Russian People* hadn't been the one-flop-too-many after all. We were going to do another one.

We read about it the next day in one of the gossip columns. Joe came in with the afternoon dailies and said resignedly:

"Terry scooped her own press department again."

She was always scooping us. She never told us anything about a new production for fear we'd tell somebody. (In the theatre, everything is a secret.) Then she'd go and confide in some columnist. It appeared that between acts of *The Russian People* on opening night, she'd told a columnist — in strictest confidence — that the composer and librettist had finished the new Guild opera and that it was to be called *Away We Go.*

Down the hall in his cage, Jack, the auditor, floating on a sea of unpaid bills, shouted at anybody who went past:

"What do they think they're producing an opera with? What're they using for money?"

and the question was indeed pertinent. During the next few weeks we heard they were holding backers' auditions, and that they had the promise of a third of the money needed, from Broadway's biggest single backer, though there were several ifs attached to his promise.

The New Year set in, *The Russian People* closed and the management plunged on with *Away We Go.* By the end of January, Joe and I had all the names connected with it.

It wasn't your normal operatic cast. The male lead was to be sung by a young man who'd played the juvenile in *Yesterday's Magic* and the singing comedienne was the ingenue from *Papa Is*

All. Both were unknown, of course. The leading comic was very well known in the Yiddish Art Theatre but hadn't done much in English.

The score had been composed by the leftover halves of two teams: an operetta lyricist whose composer partner had just died, and a musical-comedy composer whose lyricist partner had died. Add a Russian ballerina and an Armenian director from Hollywood, and our American Folk Opera was all set.

During February, people from other floors drifted into our office with progress reports. This was, they informed us, the damnedest musical anybody'd ever hatched for a sophisticated Broadway audience. It was so pure you could stage it at a church social. It opened with a middle-aged farm woman sitting alone on a bare stage churning butter, and from then on it got cleaner. They did not feel a long sequence of arty dancing was likely to improve matters on the farm.

The purity complained of was obvious on the day of the dress parade. As the girls walked across the stage in their period farm dresses, not an ankle or an upper arm was visible. I don't even remember seeing a neck. As I left the theatre, I heard Lawrence suggest to the costumer that the dresses might be cut a little lower here and there without spoiling the authenticity.

The show was to open in New Haven early in March and Joe went up a few days before the opening to "beat the drum" for it. He was very worried. Not about the show. Joe admitted frankly that there was still some work to be done on it, but he believed that by the time it opened in New York it would be the greatest show since *Hamlet.* What worried him was that some drama editor, or some columnist's assistant like Winchell's Rose, would sneak up to New Haven and see the show before it was Ready. As of now, Joe did not feel it was Ready.

(It was always a producer's worry that somebody in a newspaper's drama department would sneak out of town to a pre-Broadway tryout and write a report that would kill the show before it ever opened. But no drama department editor scared them half as much as Winchell's Rose. Walter Winchell's column appeared in cities across the country, including all the Guild's subscription cities, and was immensely influential. If Winchell's Rose — she must have had a last name but I never heard her called anything but Winchell's Rose — snuck out of town to see the tryout, the effect might be devastating.)

Away We Go opened in New Haven to mild but approving notices. Pleasant, pretty musical, they said; which cheered us. But about midafternoon, a newspaper reporter phoned and left word for Joe to call him as soon as he got back from New Haven. He said he had an important item for Joe; he didn't sound as if it were anything pleasant.

Joe came back to town, full of enthusiasm. The show, he assured us, was great. It had a few weak spots but they'd all be strengthened in Boston. Some wiseacre from an afternoon daily *had* snuck up from New York and had said bluntly the show was corn and wouldn't last a week on Broadway. But, said Joe, Terry and Lawrence were not worried. They knew they had a hit.

Lois gave him the reporter's message and Joe returned the call. He listened for a few minutes, thanked the reporter and hung up. Then he told us the news. According to the reporter, Winchell's Rose had gone to New Haven and seen the show and had wired Winchell her report on it. The wire had read:

NO LEGS NO JOKES NO CHANCE.

Winchell had shown the wire to the backer who had promised a third of the financing; and as a result, the backer was pulling his money out of the show.

Joe called Terry and Lawrence in New Haven. They'd heard about the telegram. Joe didn't mention the backer and neither did they. How they expected to finance the Broadway opening we didn't know, but when Joe left for Boston the show was still scheduled to open there the following Monday and in New York two weeks later. The show opened in Boston to fair notices — not nearly as good as those Boston had given some of our other flops and certainly not notices you could get last-minute financing on. So we still didn't know how the show was to open in New York till Jack tossed us the news casually with our mail the next morning: Terry and Lawrence had sold the Guild Theatre and building to a radio network. *Away We Go* would open on March 31, as scheduled.

Joe phoned from Boston with instructions about the opening-night press release to be sent to 10,000 Guild subscribers. He said that the whole second act had been thrown out, and that the company was working round the clock on a new second act. With a new second act, Joe felt, it would really be a great show.

For the next few days, Lois and I were busy addressing envelopes and grinding out 10,000 copies of the press release on the mimeograph machine to tell the world about the new American Folk Opera, *Away We Go*. We had about 8,000 mimeographed when Joe came back from Boston and broke the news to us that we'd have to throw them all away and start over. There had been a title change.

Nobody, it seemed, liked the title *Away We Go*. The composer had wanted to change it to *Yessirree*, but Joe was thankful to report he'd been talked out of it. The title finally agreed upon — thanks largely to Armina Marshall, Lawrence's wife, who came from out that way — was *Oklahoma.*

It sounds fine to you; you're used to it. But do me a favor and imagine you're working in a theatre and somebody tells you your new musical is to be called "New Jersey." Or "Maine." To us, "Oklahoma" remained the name of a state, even after we'd mimeographed 10,000 new releases and despite the fact that "Oklahoma" appeared three times on each one.

We had folded several hundred of them when the call came from Boston. Joe picked up the phone and we heard him say,

"Yes, Terry," and "All right, dear," and then he hung up. And then he looked at us, in the dazed way people who worked at the Guild frequently looked at each other.

"They want," he said in a faraway voice, "an exclamation point after 'Oklahoma.' "

Which is how it happened that, far into the night, Lois and I, bundled in our winter coats, sat in the outer office putting 30,000 exclamation points on 10,000 press releases, while Joe, in the inner office, bundled in his overcoat, phoned all over town hunting down and waking up various printing firms and sign painters. We were bundled in our coats because the heat had been turned off by an economy-minded management now happily engaged in spending several thousand dollars to alter houseboards, playbills, ads, three-sheet posters and souvenir booklets, to put an exclamation point after "Oklahoma."

We were not sold out for the opening, New York subscribers having dwindled to a handful after sixteen flops. Nor did we get any help from the weather. When I woke on the morning of March 31, with a cold, it was snowing.

By six that evening, the snow had turned to sleet and my cold included a cough. As I left the office to go home and climb into a drafty evening dress, Joe took pity on me.

"I don't need you there, dear," he said. "Don't come unless you feel like it."

I felt guilty about not going as I ate a quick dinner in a cafeteria. But by the time I'd fought my way home through the sleet guilt had given way to self-preservation. I undressed and crawled thankfully into bed. In bed, I reached for the wet newspaper I'd brought home and opened it to the theatre page. Our big opening-night ad leaped out at me: *"Oklahoma!"*

Slowly, surely, with that foggy bewilderment you were bound to feel sooner or later if you worked at the Theatre Guild long enough, I saw that Terry and Lawrence were right. About the exclamation point.

I did not allow myself to speculate on the insane possibility that they might also be right about such brainwaves as a clean, corn-fed musical with no legs and no jokes and with a score by Richard Rodgers and Oscar Hammerstein II, who'd never collaborated before; a full-blown ballet by an unknown young choreographer named Agnes de Mille; and a cast of unknowns, including Celeste Holm, the ingenue from *Papa Is All*.

I switched off the lamp, thinking how typical it was of both this epic and the Guild that the notices would appear on the morning of April Fool's Day. I coughed, pulled up the blankets and, as I drifted off to sleep, said a silent Good Luck to Alfred Drake, the juvenile from *Yesterday's Magic*, who was at that moment strolling out onto the stage of the St. James Theatre, singing:

"Oh, what a beautiful morning!"

· 8 ·

Large Furnished Rear with Kitchen Privileges

WHEN A YOUNG WRITER SETS OUT for New York to crash the theatre, she is prepared to starve in a garret for a while. She has read
the solemn pronouncement of a turn-of-the-century writer named
Richard Harding Davis, that "a man who can afford a hall bedroom in New York City is better off than he would be if he owned
160 acres of prairie." She has seen *La Bohème* and wept as
Rodolfo gallantly tossed his poems into the fire to warm his garret
on Christmas Eve. And she has seen *Stage Door* — both Broadway
and film versions — describing life at the Rehearsal Club, a female
"residence club" where young actresses bolster each other's mor-
ale in charming dormitory rooms. She has gathered from all of
these testimonials that starving in a garret is a rich, purifying
experience, and she wants it. And she gets it.

And of course, *after* she gets it, it dawns on her that when
Richard Harding Davis wrote that a New York hall bedroom was
better than 160 acres of prairie he was no longer living in a New
York hall bedroom, having grown rich enough to afford a town
house and nostalgia; she types her play huddled in blankets and
sourly informs Rodolfo he should be damn glad he's got a fireplace
to throw his poems into; and she thinks that somebody in *Stage
Door* might have mentioned that the Rehearsal Club has a special

New York electrical system known as DC — direct current — which means that the day she moves in she's going to blow her radio, her iron, and all the building's fuses, and that while the fuses can be fixed, her radio and iron can't, which in turn means that till next Christmas she's going to have to do without a radio, press her skirts under the mattress, and iron her scarves, blouses and handkerchiefs by pasting them soaking wet to a mirror.

My first garret — not counting the Rehearsal Club, which took me in temporarily as a favor to Terry and kept me just long enough to ruin my appliances — was one of those hall bedrooms Richard Harding Davis was so crazy about. This was way back in my fellowship year. I rented a hall bedroom on the fifth floor of a brownstone walk-up rooming house on West Sixty-ninth Street. The upper West Side was lined with four- and five-story brownstone houses built in the 1880s as homes for the well-to-do. Fifty or sixty years later the houses were moldering, vermin-ridden rooming houses. Ours had a cavernous entrance hall and a great, gloomy, unlit staircase, the steps adorned with dirty shreds of ancient carpeting and creaking eerily all the way up — and if you passed a dead rat on the stairs you were just very thankful he was dead.

I used to creak my way up four flights each night, grope down the musty hall to the third room on the left, unlock the door, feel for the string attached to the twenty-five-watt bulb overhead and ask myself why I'd left Philadelphia.

My room looked out on a stone wall and I couldn't see to comb my hair, let alone type my play, so I went out and bought a seventy-five-watt bulb and climbed on a chair and several of my best books to install it. But when I came home that night, the seventy-five-watter was gone and the twenty-five-watter was back. Forced to take the landlady's hint about saving electricity, I told myself Shakespeare probably never used more than twenty-five candles at a time either.

The room had a chair, a dresser and a bed. Some of the rooms

"I'm takin' you to a woman's hotel," he said. "It ain't the Ritz but it's respectable. You stay there till you know your way around. Hear?"

The hotel room cost eleven dollars a week, more than a third of my weekly thirty-dollar fellowship allowance. But if the room was as small and narrow as a convent cell it was also as clean. I crawled thankfully into bed and went to sleep.

When I surveyed the lobby the next morning I seemed to be the only guest in the hotel who was under sixty-five. This had one unfortunate consequence which I got used to. My dates never did, however.

A man from the seminar took me out one Saturday night and when he brought me home he walked me to the elevator, where we had to say good night since Men Were Not Allowed Above the Mezzanine. The elevator arrived, and as my escort leaned over to kiss me good night, two black-suited men stepped out of the elevator carrying a sack between them.

Old ladies were carried out of there at the rate of a sack a month — always late at night, and somehow I was always around to assist. Me and my date. The next morning there'd be a sign on the lobby bulletin board:

"FOR SALE: Matched luggage." Or "Caracul coat. Good condition." I took advantage of one of those sales to throw out my camp duffel bag. I bought a wardrobe trunk for eight dollars, in case one of my plays ever went touring.

From then on, I alternated between small hotel rooms and larger rooming-house rooms that were somehow always on the top floor of a walk-up where you trudged up four double flights of stairs and, with your foot on the top step, remembered you were out of cigarettes. Both the hotel manager and the rooming-house landlady locked you out of your room if they caught you using a hot plate to save the price of a cafeteria breakfast.

All this time I cherished the dream of finding the ideal garret, a room large and light enough to work in and with what I described to myself as "hot plate privileges." But a year after *Oklahoma!* opened, the need for such a room became acute. I left the Guild and took a part-time job which would give me more time for my playwriting (see next chapter), but this meant that I'd be working at home and earning less. In the narrow hotel room I was living in that season, I scanned the Furnished Rooms columns in *The Times* without finding anything suitable I could afford. And then, one bright morning, there it was:

> Lg. furn. rear. Share bath.
> Kitch. priv. $40 monthly.

Since I'd had to slog out to the nearest cafeteria for breakfast every morning for five years, rain, sleet or cold-in-the-head — which is a very good way to feel sorry for yourself, especially on a rainy Sunday — "kitchen privileges" was the pot of gold at the end of the rainbow.

I hurried around to the address given, on a quiet upper East Side street. The building was a narrow greystone, sandwiched in between a vegetable market and a handsome, discreetly anonymous building on the corner.

I found the super and asked about the furnished rear. He said it had already been rented, but a large furnished front had just come vacant for a few dollars more. It was on the top floor and we rode up in an undreamed-of elevator to look at it. It was a big, sunny room with a studio couch, an armchair, and a table big enough to accommodate my typewriter during the day and two dinner guests in the evening.

The super led me halfway down the hall to show me the bathroom and then on down to the far end of the hall and into a big old kitchen with an assortment of battered community pots and pans; and I knew I was home. He explained that I would share the it down and went on having open discussions, attended by all five tenants and an increasing number of cockroaches.

That was a great kitchen for signs.

> I accidentally overturned the sugar bowl on the middle shelf of the right-hand cabinet.
> I cleaned it up.
> I will replace sugar if owner will see me.
>
> FLORRIE.

> Please leave this oven at 350 degrees until my casserole is done.
> I will take it out at five o'clock.
>
> M.E.B.

> PLEASE MOVE THIS COFFEE POT ONTO YOUR CLOSET SHELF. IT CAN NOT STAND ON THIS BURNER ALL DAY. OTHER PEOPLE ARE ENTITLED TO USE THIS BURNER.
>
> (unsigned)

Maudiebird caused a whole series of kitchen spats because her room was next to the kitchen. She ate her meager supper early and generally retired to her room with it just as the rest of us arrived in the kitchen to start our dinners. If one of us sang or laughed or spoke above a library whisper, Birdie was sure to appear in the doorway and say that we would have to stop making so much noise, she was working on her figures.

"How long can it take her," I demanded when she'd gone back to her room, "to add up twenty hours of companion-sitting and six hours of park-bench–sitting?"

And Florrie, when anybody laughed, would mutter:

"Be quiet: Birdie's doing her Examples."

The bathroom crises were caused entirely by Gale and me.

I mentioned that there was a discreetly anonymous building next door to us on the corner. It was six stories high, so that our seventh-floor bathroom overlooked its roof. Gale and I, through the bathroom window, had made the acquaintance of two young men who sunbathed on the roof occasionally, after their work in the discreet building, which was a very upper-class funeral parlor. One Saturday afternoon not long after I moved in, Gale and I were washing our hair and doing our nails in the bathroom when one of the boys called up to us:

"Have you girls got dates for tonight?" For a wonder, we both did.

"Would you like some flowers to wear?" he inquired. We said we'd love some and the boy told us he'd be right back. He and his friend disappeared and came back five minutes later carrying between them a blanket of gardenias.

"Compliments of the corpse!" one of the boys said cheerily. "They came too late for the funeral."

They upended the gardenia blanket and hoisted it up and Gale and I leaned down and hauled it up and through the window.

Honesty compels me to admit that he did not say "the corpse," he told us *whose* corpse. It was the body of a distinguished statesman and if I wasn't afraid the funeral parlor would sue me I'd tell you his name. Gale and I were reluctant to steal his flowers but the boys explained that famous corpses often got flowers from total strangers, with cards reading "An Admirer," "An Unknown Friend," and so forth; and when these offerings were too ostentatious or came too late for the funeral, the family of the deceased directed that the flowers be sent to some hospital. Several hospitals having done very well by this particular corpse, the boys saw no reason to consult the family about giving us one gardenia blanket.

Thus reassured, Gale and I sat down on the bathroom floor to detach ourselves a pair of corsages. Let me tell you it was no easy trick. Each flower was wired to the greenery with heavy wire and you nearly ripped your fingers off detaching a corsage spray. It therefore took us some time — and of course, while we were working, there was an importunate knock on the bathroom door.

"Let's carry it to my room," I said to Gale.

"I am not," she said in her Texas drawl, "paradin' through the hall with a funeral blanket on my head."

Instead, she turned on the bath faucets to indicate we'd be in there for some time. This brought a stream of French invective from Mamselle, so as soon as I heard her door slam, I tiptoed out of the bathroom with the blanket in my arms, and when I'd made it safely to my room, Gale called loudly to the rest of the hall:

"Bathroom's free!"

and we finished our corsages in my room.

During the single season the two boys worked next door, we had perfectly glorious flowers to wear and bowls of lilies as centerpieces for our dinette tables. We also got mildly ghoulish. I'd read in *The Times* that a certain famous actress had died and was on view at our parlor, and I'd hurry down the hall, knock on Gale's door and when she opened it cry: "Guess who's next door!"

All in all, it was garret living at its best, and it was a sad day for all of us when we received notice that the building was to be renovated and we'd have to move.

This was 1948, and there was a severe postwar housing shortage in New York. Gale and I each found a friend willing to take us in temporarily; Florrie moved in with her recently widowed sister; Mamselle's school found her a room in a residence club; and Maudiebird, after three months of searching, finally found a fourth-floor walk-up. It gave me a pang to think of her thin old legs climbing four flights several times a day, but she told me wistfully that a room in an elevator building was too expensive for anybody.

We bade each other farewell and went our separate ways. My way took me into the sharp teeth of the housing shortage. The friend who took me in had barely helped me get settled in her apartment when it was completely gutted by fire. The next day I was out on the street with my salvageable clothes in a suitcase in one hand and my portable typewriter in the other, looking for a place to live.

Whole families were living in their cars that year. I met them on Saturday nights when all of us who were homeless gathered at *The New York Times* office to get the earliest edition of the Sunday real estate section. During the next eighteen months I had eleven addresses, most of them two-week and one-month sublets from people going on winter or summer vacations. When there was no sublet I slept at Maxine's — she had twin beds in her room — until I became so acutely embarrassed at seeming to move in on her that I couldn't bring myself to do it one more night and paid a doorman to let me sleep on two lobby chairs instead.

So you'll understand that when, after eighteen homeless months, I finally found a "converted apartment" available, I was past caring that the rent was twice what I could afford.

The building was a five-story greystone on East Ninety-fifth Street and had formerly been a private home. Its larger rooms had been "converted" to apartments by installing ancient kitchen and bathroom equipment in adjoining smaller rooms. The ground-floor apartment I looked at was a large, dark room-in-the-back, its one window looking out on a courtyard below and a stone wall opposite. Beyond it, the kitchen with its ancient stove and leaky refrigerator was all mine, and the adjoining bare room with its iron tub and a chain toilet in a former closet was the first private bathroom of my life. And no mansion could have seemed more beautiful to me than that three-room hovel when I was told it might be mine.

It wasn't mine for certain. The tenant who was moving out told me his lease had only a month to run and he couldn't guarantee the rental agency would give me a new lease. I wanted to go directly to the building's owner but of course that wasn't possible.

When I went down to see the rental agent, he explained that the owner owned several similar buildings and had nothing to do with the running of any of them. Everything was handled by the agency. But the rental agent was kind and said that if my references were satisfactory he saw no reason why I shouldn't count on a lease. I had to be content with that.

I moved in forthwith and plunged into the job of furnishing and decorating. I furnished the room in what New Yorkers called Early Orange Crate. The super helped me make a bookcase out of wooden planks he found in the cellar, and a dressing table for the bathroom out of an orange crate. One of my brothers donated a dresser his little girls had outgrown, and I bought a secondhand dropleaf table and chairs and a secondhand studio bed. Add white enamel paint to cover everything, my old white rug, and yards of red burlap which Maxine draped across the top of the window and down over the rusty living-room pipes in an opulent swag — and in our objective opinion the room was simply stunning.

Two thorny problems remained. The kitchen and bathroom floors were covered with stained, faded and cracked linoleum, which clearly had to be replaced. I bought two bright rolls of linoleum at Woolworth's, brought them home — and wondered what to do with them. What did I know about cutting linoleum and running it around the kitchen pipes and bathroom pipes and under the elderly stove and bathtub? I phoned Maxine.

"How much would it cost me," I asked, "to hire a man to cut and lay new linoleum for me?"

"A fortune," said Maxine positively.

"Well, I don't know what to do!" I said. "I bought all this linoleum and I bought a knife and a ruler they said I'd need, and I'm paralyzed. I don't know where to start!"

There was a thoughtful pause at the other end.

"What night," asked Maxine, "is Tom coming for your lesson?"
Oh.

So when Tom came for my Latin lesson he spent four exhausting hours stretched out on the kitchen and bathroom floors — neither long enough to accommodate all of him, but the rooms fortunately having no door between. Armed with ruler, knife, hammer, a box of tacks and the disposition of a saint, he measured, cut and tacked my new kitchen and bathroom linoleum while I read him the Gospel According to St. Matthew out of a Latin Bible borrowed from him.

The bathroom floor looked so bright and new it called attention to the dirty, faded wallpaper. So a week later, when Tom arrived for my lesson, he found the bathtub full of water and two rolls of do-it-yourself wallpaper waiting for him, and he put in another active recreational evening wallpapering the bathroom while I read to him out of my Catullus.

The last remaining problem concerned kitchen equipment; and it was in her solution to this one that Maxine pulled off her greatest financial coup.

Never having owned a kitchen before, I made the appalling discovery that except for a coffee pot and a few plates left over from the seventh-floor garret, I had nothing whatsoever to put in it. I mean I didn't own a strainer, a kitchen fork or spoon, a pot holder, a can opener, a pot or a pan. Nothing. I sat down and made a list of bare kitchen essentials and when I totted up the approximate cost the total came to roughly fifty dollars.

If I have to add this, I didn't have fifty dollars.

Maxine and I were going to theatre that night and we met at a nearby drugstore for our watch-and-wait cup of coffee.

"Do we have a problem!" I said as we ordered the coffee. I gave her my kitchen list, with the total cost at the bottom ringed round with exclamation points.

Our coffee came and Maxine sipped hers absently as she studied the list.

"What you need," she said finally, "is a kitchen shower."

"I'm not getting married," I said.

"You're marrying New York," said Maxine. "You'll have to

write a cute invitation. We'll have the shower at my house. A luncheon. A Saturday luncheon."

"I couldn't!" I said. "I can't send out invitations asking people to furnish my kitchen!"

"You're not sending the invitations. I'm sending them. You don't know anything about the luncheon," said Maxine. "It's a surprise. Showers are always surprises. You're just coming to my house for lunch. When you get there, be surprised."

We drew up the invitation in the theatre lobby during intermission. We drew up a list of guests, including my two out-of-town sisters-in-law who, said Maxine, wouldn't come but wouldn't-have-the-nerve-not-to-send-something. And to avoid duplication, Maxine had me draw up an alphabetical list of essential items, a copy of which she enclosed with each invitation, together with a request that the recipient check off the item she was bringing.

And so on the appointed Saturday I wandered into Maxine's parents' apartment for lunch — and there was my sister-in-law come all the way in from Garden City and a simple host of friends. And sitting in the middle of the floor in a large wicker basket, each item brightly wrapped and tied with flossy ribbon, were frying pans and double boilers and mixing bowls and kitchen knives and pot holders and dish towels and a roasting pan and a Revere Ware teakettle that sang.

By the end of the month I had as warm and bright and well-equipped a home as any penniless writer ever had. And none of it securely mine until I signed a lease.

On the day the old lease ran out, I went down to the rental office ready to do battle but inwardly terrified, with the eighteen-month nightmare fresh in my memory.

To my relief, the agent smiled warmly at me when I walked into his office. He told me that my references had been approved and that my lease was ready for signing. I sat down, suddenly weak. The agent pushed the lease toward me and handed me a pen. I didn't even read the lease, I'd have signed anything that guaranteed a roof over my head. I went straight to the bottom of the page, where the two lines for signatures were: the bottom line marked OWNER, the top line marked TENANT. I signed my name along the line marked TENANT.

Then the pen slipped out of my hand and rolled to the floor and I stared at the lease, dumbfounded. Because on the line marked OWNER, a signature had been written just below my own. In a thin spidery hand, it read:

"Maude E. Bird."

·9·

Outside Hollywood

To BE YOUNG and trying to crash the theatre in the forties was to resign yourself to the chronic problem of how to earn enough money to keep alive till you became famous on Broadway. You learned to avoid nine-to-five jobs and look instead for part-time work which, though it paid a meager wage, would leave you free most of the day to pursue what you liked to think of as your real profession.

The jobs actors took in those days ran a gamut considerably longer than this book. An actor, for instance, might work as a bellhop, bartender, bus driver, barker on a sightseeing bus, bonded messenger, bouncer, or butcher's delivery boy, and that's only the B's.

Actresses were more limited, as Maxine discovered, even though when she filled out an Employment Agency Questionnaire and came to the question: "Kind of Position Wanted:_____" she wrote simply: "I'll do anything." In addition to taking street-corner and door-to-door surveys, Maxine drove a school bus, was a saleslady at Lord & Taylor during the pre-Christmas rush, and taught elocution in a convent.

Maxine's trouble was that when she was out of work she got impetuous and she'd seize any job that came along without a careful enough consideration of the hours involved. There was the winter she drove the school bus, for instance. Like most actresses, she was used to going to bed very late and sleeping half the morning. Even when she wasn't in a play, she was generally up half the night working on some big project like drying her hair.

Since Maxine's hair was shoulder-length and as thick as a mop, just washing it took most of the evening. And for reasons known to nobody, she decided that the way to dry it was to turn on the oven, sit on the kitchen floor and spread her hair out on an oven rack to dry. She put the oven on at the lowest possible heat so as not to set her hair on fire, and as a result it took her half the night to dry it. She washed it once a week, sat with her hair in the oven till two or three in the morning and as a result slept through the alarm clock five hours later.

So during the season when she drove the school bus, she overslept regularly one morning a week, thereby leaving twenty-five children standing around under twenty-five apartment-house canopies waiting for the school bus. And at least one afternoon a week she was summoned to a two o'clock audition which invariably started an hour late and ran longer than anticipated, causing her to leave twenty-five children standing on the school steps for a couple of hours waiting for the bus to take them home. So Maxine and the school parted company by mutual consent after three months, freeing her in time for the Christmas rush at Lord & Taylor.

Ideally, of course, she found what might be called grey-area acting jobs, like appearing in that U.S. government–sponsored documentary on gonorrhea which enabled her to be seen by thousands of American GIs during World War II.

But the best part-time job for an actress was a running part in a radio soap opera, which was acting of a sort and the easiest imaginable (you didn't have to memorize lines, you just read them), and which paid handsomely. Maxine hit this jackpot only once. For a halcyon thirteen weeks she was Caroline, the female menace in The Romance of Helen Trent. Unfortunately, by the end of thirteen weeks Maxine had had radio, and radio, she was frank to admit, had had her.

"I'm standing there in front of the mike," she reported to me over coffee at the Astor drugstore after her first broadcast, "I'm enunciating beautifully and giving a magnificently bitchy performance, as called for — when I notice that the idiot director is staring at me and making little-bitty circles with his thumbs, both thumbs going round and round and round. I tried to ignore him but he went on staring at me, making more and more little-bitty circles in the air with his thumbs. And I said to myself: 'That man is getting on my nerves.'

"So as soon as I had a ten-second pause, I turned to him and mouthed silently: 'Stop doing that.' And I shook the script at him for emphasis, only the script accidentally hit the microphone causing a needle to fly up to the top which meant that on millions of radios across the country, The Romance of Helen Trent was instantly drowned out by static."

After the broadcast she learned that the little circles were radio sign language for "Speed it up." It was some weeks before she learned the sign for "Slow down."

"Can they write 'Slow down' on a piece of paper and hand it to you?" she demanded of me as we sat on stools in Sardi's bar, where she was putting her radio profits to good use by being Seen. "No! When they want you to slow down, the director stares at you with his fists close together against his chest and then slowly pulls his fists away from each other — like a Stanislavski improvisation of a taffy-pull. This means s-t-r-e-t-c-h in radio, but nobody tells you this, you have to guess it! I'm standing there trying to give a performance and I see him step in front of me and start pulling his fists apart and I think: 'In the middle of a radio broadcast, he has to start playing The Game!'" (The Game is what theatre people call Charades.)

So what with one thing and another, Maxine wasn't greatly surprised one day, just before the expiration of her thirteen-week contract, to read in the script that Caroline's headaches had definitely been diagnosed as an obscure form of Rocky Mountain fever which she could cure only by moving to Switzerland for several years. Her contract was not renewed, the party was over and a week later she was back at her old post in front of Radio City Music Hall, taking surveys on the average woman's opinion of hormone creams and what a man looks for in a razor blade.

Playwrights, of course, hunted for writing jobs. For a while I thought I had the best of these, writing publicity in the Theatre Guild press department. But the Guild job took the whole day and occasional evenings, leaving me no time to write in. So eventually I left the Guild and began looking for part-time jobs instead. Fortunately, back in the forties, there was one part-time job for which would-be playwrights and novelists were in demand.

This was the era when Hollywood was in its heyday, and the best of all part-time writing jobs was to be had in the New York offices of Hollywood studios. Warner's, 20th Century-Fox, M-G-M, Columbia, Paramount, Selznick, Universal, all had New York story departments which became a positive Mecca for unemployed, undiscovered writers.

I got to Mecca through a letter from the story editor at one of the studios. He wrote to say he'd read my play and had recommended me to the West Coast office as a writer the studio might want at some future date. I wrote back and said How about a part-time job with the East Coast office now instead? Two days later I was an outside reader for a studio we'll call Monograph.

There were inside readers and outside readers and I'll explain the whole thing to you in a minute, but first I would like you to appreciate what people with that job title had to contend with. Some tax expert or friend of your family would ask:

"What do you do for a living?"
and you'd say:

"I'm an outside reader for a film studio"
and the questioner would give you the blankest look ever seen on a human face and say:

"You're a what?"
and you knew it would take you twenty minutes to explain it, and there was no way you could avoid explaining it, and in four or five years you got so *tired* explaining it.

Most Hollywood movies were adapted from novels, plays and short stories which the studios bought by the ton. To find this material, every studio hired inside readers, who worked nine-to-five in the studio offices; and outside readers, who worked part-time and at home. We didn't go out and look for the material, you understand; we read what was submitted to the studio by producers and publishers, playbrokers and literary agents, magazines and newspapers. The submissions included plays, novels, short stories, science fiction, and westerns and whodunits by the gross. Every reader had a specialty — mine was plays — but when your specialty wasn't available you read whatever was. Sooner or later, you read everything imaginable and a lot that wasn't.

The studios were supposed to accept manuscripts only from professional sources but it never worked out that way. If the story editor's mother's janitor wrote a play, Monograph covered it. If your landlady or your Aunt Clara thought her life would make a book and wrote the book in six hundred pages, as long as the pages were typed she could submit it and Monograph would cover it. It didn't have to be literate, it didn't have to be sane, it just had to be typed.

We went to Monograph at four each afternoon, got a play or novel, took it home and read it, wrote a two-page Summary and a Comment and brought the work in at four the next afternoon. I can't print a two-page Summary here but a friend of mine still at Monograph dug a couple of my old Comments out of the files as samples for you, to indicate the extent of what Monograph covered. Comments were readers' opinions of the work covered and looked like this:

TITLE: Hope Is Eternal
AUTHOR: John Malan
FORM: Playscript

COMMENT:

Crackpot illiterate fantasy about an unsuccessful playwright who throws himself under a subway train, wakes up in Heaven and finds himself posthumously famous on Broadway. (I've tried everything else; next year I may try this.)

TITLE: Cappy Meets the Test
AUTHOR: Frances Eager Dawes
FORM: Juvenile (8–12 age group)

COMMENT:

If Cappy doesn't straighten out and pass his algebra test, Hilldale High is going to lose the championship football game. Listen, this is my second Eager Dawes this week, next week it's somebody else's turn, O.K.?

For reading and summarizing a play or novel you got $6 (in 1947 when I started reading). The next year they raised it to $8 and by the early fifties (when I quit) it had got up to $10. You read one a day and two or three over a weekend. You weren't supposed to read for two studios at once — it was like working for both Macy's and Gimbel's — but when the bills piled up you bootlegged a little reading from a second studio. And you went baby-sitting, evenings, and read Monograph's scripts on the baby's family's electric bill, and they also had to give you dinner half the time, and one way or another if you didn't exactly make a living you somehow made out.

Once you learned the technique of professional reading, you

had the whole day free to write in. I could read a long novel in an evening, write the summary of it after breakfast and at nine-thirty be free to write until four, when I took the work in to Monograph. I keep hearing about these expensive courses that will teach you how to read faster. Don't take them; I'll give you the whole course right here, free. The technique is never to be applied to books you want to read, you understand; it's only for books you don't want to read but have to.

Open to page one of a long novel you don't want to read, and run your eye down the left-hand side of the page, noting the first sentence in each paragraph. Say a paragraph begins:

"The house was set well back, in . . ."

Skip the whole paragraph; it's going to describe the house and grounds and you're not reading the book for the architecture. Run your eye on down to the paragraph beginning:

"Her eyes were a pale watery blue. Her skin, which had once . . ." Skip that paragraph too; she's getting old and unattractive. You've learned this in a sentence-and-a-half, why read twelve?

Skip the paragraph beginning:

"He strode toward the moors. In the darkening light, the moors . . ." unless you're just crazy about moors.

Keep running your eye down past all such paragraphs until you come to a paragraph in which something *happens*. Say you come to a murder or a rape on page 250. You can count on the author spending at least thirty pages on this event. The facts will be set forth on pages 250–251, the outcome will be found on pages 279–280. Skip the pages in between; the studio that hired you only wants the facts and you only want to get to bed before dawn.

When reading plays, skip the parentheses.

"(Large, well-appointed living room. At left . . .)" It goes on for ten or twenty lines and you've read the only one the set designer will pay any attention to.

"(JANE *enters through French windows.* SHE *is a tall, rather . . .*)"
She's tall unless the director happens to cast a short actress for the
part.

After the first scene, the parentheses will include all the emo-
tions the playwright couldn't manage to convey in the dialogue.
It's easier, for instance, to write "*(angrily)*" than it is to write an
angry line. Skip all those, too; the audience won't see them and
every actor and actress I ever knew found them distracting and
blacked them out before learning the part.

Of course, when we got a new Steinbeck or Hemingway novel,
or a Williams or Miller play, we didn't write a two-page summary, we wrote a ten-to-twenty-page synopsis, including all the
minor characters and large hunks of dialogue; but long synopses
paid a dollar a page so they were worth the time they took.

Every afternoon at four o'clock, the outside readers took their
completed assignments down to the Broadway theatre district
(where most studios had their offices) and up to the Monograph
story department, which occupied half a floor in an office building
and was just jumping with personnel.

There was the story editor, in charge of novels; the play editor,
in charge of plays; their assistant, who assigned work to the readers; Jean, in charge of cataloguing and returning all material
submitted; Lilian, who sent copies of all readers' reports to Monograph's Hollywood office; and Evelyn, who got out a news bulletin on what everybody else was doing. Not forgetting two
private secretaries, an at-large stenographer and Miriam, the file
clerk. And way down at the end of a hall, in a private dungeon of
their own, were the inside readers who read all day long. We
never saw them; they never came out.

The outside readers sat in a row on a bench outside the assistant's office, each of us waiting our turn to go in. All of us were
starving writers except Dolly. And my God, how we resented
Dolly.

Dolly was a fashionable young matron who came to Monograph looking and behaving as if she were at a glamorous cocktail party. Her husband was a successful businessman and Dolly didn't need the reading job. She read for fun — she told us with entire innocence that she thought reading was "a fun job." And wouldn't you know Dolly's specialty was the easiest and best-paid of all reading work? She read the empty little romances in women's magazines — *Ladies' Home Journal, Woman's Home Companion, Good Housekeeping* — which in those days published only creampuff fiction. Six stories to a magazine, Dolly got $2 per story and only had to write one-paragraph summaries on little file cards.

Dolly would sit on that bench with a fur stole across her lap and say chattily to all us hungry writers:

"I didn't feel like taking any work last night. But yesterday morning I saw a pair of alligator pumps at Saks and I looked at the price tag and it was only two magazines! So when they asked if I wanted any work last night I said to myself: 'Dolly, you take it! You can get those alligator shoes!' So I took it."

Out of our mouths, you understand, she took it. She was a very pleasant woman, friendly and sociable; but I'd sit on that bench watching one of her two-magazine alligator pumps dangle from a nylon toe — I wore pants to Monograph myself because with pants you could wear thirty-five-cent ankle socks instead of $1.35 nylons — and wish I could hate her.

But the fact that she didn't need the job was only (a). (b) Dolly wasn't a writer. Not being a writer, she used to utter the most loathsome of all amateur literary clichés. She'd leaf through the *Ladies' Home Journal* she'd just read and she'd say:

"I could write better stories than these."

If she said it once she said it three times a week.

Understand, none of us had a high opinion of women's magazine fiction. But being writers, we knew that any kind of specialized writing demanded technical skill, at the very least. What infuriated us was that Dolly didn't know how fiendishly difficult it was to write *anything,* especially anything salable. So every time she said: "I could write better stories than these," there'd be a highly charged pause and I'd wonder if this was the day one of the male readers was finally going to go berserk and stomp her to death.

The other readers were the standard types to be found in every studio reading department. If standard is the word.

There was middle-aged Miss Manheimer, who was large and stout and addicted to garden hats with bunches of fruit on them and lived with her mother. There was Jason, a failed actor who had decided to be a playwright instead. And there was Wide-Margin Wirtz, who was bald and fat and the reading department thief.

Readers were permitted to do a long synopsis (which paid ten to twenty dollars) whenever they considered a manuscript warranted it. Wide-Margin thought everything he read warranted it. But he didn't exactly write a ten-page synopsis. What he did was set three-inch margins at both ends of the typewriter so that his synopsis ran like a wide ribbon down the center of the paper, stretching two or three pages of copy to ten. Now and then the editors would complain and Wide-Margin would sulk along on six-dollar summaries until the fuss died down. Then he'd start again. But that's not what I meant by "thief."

I ran out of paper in the middle of a long synopsis one morning and since Wide-Margin lived closer to me than any of the other readers I phoned to ask him if he had any extra "setups" — paper with carbon attached — and he said he had plenty so I went over to his apartment to get them. He was typing when I got there, and he waved toward a closet and said:

"Help yourself."

I opened the closet door and what met my eyes was a writer's dream of Christmas morning. On shelves from floor to ceiling were reams of Monograph typing paper and setups, boxes of carbon paper, typewriter ribbons, pens, pencils, rubber bands, paper clips and two stapling machines. Monograph eventually caught him raiding the supply room and fired him and he moved on to another studio.

But our prize character was Winston Atterbury. Winston was Monograph's disappearing reader.

Every studio had for its sins one reader to whom it gave the galleys of, say, *The Rise and Fall of the Third Reich*. That is, it was always a big book, six or seven hundred pages long, it was always a widely heralded work by an important writer, it was still in printer's galleys and no other studio had yet seen it. The galleys had been stolen from the publisher's office by bribing a stenographer or office boy, and rushed to the studio late on a Friday afternoon. The reader was summoned, taken into the story editor's private office, told about the property and exhorted to read the book over the weekend taking copious notes, do a long synopsis later for double money, but rush the galleys back to Monograph early Monday morning so they could be whipped over to the publisher's office before they were missed. The reader would nod eagerly, hurry home with the galleys and disappear from the face of the earth for two weeks.

That's a disappearing reader. And I have to say that during four or five years of reading for a living, almost every reader was tempted to disappear at least once. Including me.

I've never liked novels and there were weeks when I had to read one a night for Monograph. But I was usually spared what I regarded as the ultimate professional-reading horror: the seven-hundred-page, three-generation family saga that always had more subplots than a soap opera and more characters than Dickens, and forced you to make pages and pages of notes. Anything worse was simply beyond my imagination.

Well, on the blackest Friday I ever want to see, I was summoned to Monograph and handed three outsized paperback volumes of an English book which was about to be published here. I was to read all three volumes over the weekend, and since each volume was double the length of the usual novel I was invited to charge double money for each. I hurried home with the three volumes and after dinner began to read Volume I. And if Monograph's office had been open at that hour, I'd have phoned and quit my job.

What I had to read, during that nightmare weekend — taking notes on all place names, characters' names and events therein — was fifteen hundred stupefying pages of the sticky mythology of J. R. R. Tolkein. (I hope I'm spelling his name wrong.) I remember opening one volume to a first line which read

Mr. Bilbo Baggins of Bag End announced that he would shortly be celebrating his eleventy-first birthday. . . .

and phoning several friends to say good-bye because suicide seemed so obviously preferable to five hundred more pages of that.

I also remember the bill I turned in:

For Reading and Summarizing:	
TITLE: Lord of the Rings	
AUTHOR: J. R. R. Tolkien	
Volume I	$ 20
Volume II	20
Volume III	20
Mental Torture	40
TOTAL	$100

They paid it. I think they knew how close I'd come to disappearing; and one disappearing reader per season was all any studio could cope with. We had three of them during the years I was at Monograph. Each had his own technique for evading studio attempts to find him during his disappearance. First there was

Howie, who hid out in the flophouse movie theatres lining Forty-second Street; then there was Elwood, who got friends in Chicago or Pittsburgh to send bogus telegrams to the studio reading CALLED AWAY BY DEATH IN FAMILY GALLEYS WITH LANDLADY EL-WOOD, which Monograph appreciated because they could send somebody up to the Bronx to get the galleys back. Lastly, there was Winston Atterbury.

Winston had bleached blond curls with bleached blond side-burns and he was a very dapper dresser, he favored pearl-grey ties to match his pearl-grey suede shoes. As long as I knew him he was working on a novel about plantation days in the Old South. We'd assumed he was born Willie Smith or Joe Potts and renamed himself Winston Atterbury, but during his disappearance his mother phoned from Omaha to ask if Monograph knew "where my son is," and damned if she wasn't Mrs. Atterbury.

Winston was a professional pauper. Every day, he borrowed six cents from Miriam, the file clerk. Miriam was a willowy, dark-haired girl with great sympathetic brown eyes and a heart that melted and bled for Monograph's underpaid outside readers. Her voice shook when she spoke of us because we had no union and no minimum wage and no unemployment insurance and no consid-eration from Monograph and we were all so nice and so talented and so pathetic.

So naturally it was Miriam Winston turned to when he first decided to borrow six cents. She listened with brimming eyes as he explained he only had nine cents and if he couldn't borrow six he'd have to walk to Washington Heights, where his rooming house was; it took a bus and a subway to get there.

Miriam begged him, she entreated him, to take at least a quar-ter. But no, six cents was all he would take. After that, Miriam lent him six or eight cents a day — he varied the amount but it never went above nine — and on Friday, payday, he paid her back. Then one Friday I walked into the office in time to hear

Miriam tell Winston in a low, passionate voice that she would absolutely not take his thirty-one cents, he was to use it toward a good big lamb chop.

"Why didn't you take it?" I asked her when Winston had gone. "He just got paid and we've had a good week."

Miriam turned on me, trembling with compassionate fury.

"Would you like to know," she demanded, quivering, "what that boy did for his dinner last night?"

"What did he do for his dinner last night?" I asked obligingly.

"He ate cat food!" said Miriam and burst into tears.

I couldn't say so to the mother of us all, but Winston's poverty stories never inspired much confidence in me. They were too interesting by half.

He was there quite awhile before we discovered Winston was a disappearer. He disappeared with *The Wall* by John Hersey.

The Wall was not only the hottest advance property of the year, it was also the longest. It came into the office in three hundred and thirty galleys, each galley nine feet long if it was an inch. Winston was summoned into the inner office late on a Friday afternoon and told to take copious notes on the book over the weekend and do a long synopsis at his leisure, just so he got the galleys back early Monday morning. Winston nodded eagerly, hurried home to Washington Heights and disappeared.

When he didn't show Monday morning, Monograph phoned the stationery store on the corner next to his rooming house (the rooming house had no phone) and asked the owner to call Winston to the phone. The owner sent somebody up to Winston's room but Winston wasn't there. All morning, the story editor's secretary kept on phoning without success. In the afternoon she sent Winston a telegram.

On Tuesday, two secretaries were assigned the job of locating Winston. Every hour they phoned the stationery store and got somebody to run up and knock on Winston's door and all day long he wasn't home. On Wednesday, Jason, one of the other readers, offered to go up to Washington Heights and ask the landlady to let him into Winston's room so he could get *The Wall* out of it. Off Jason went to Washington Heights and the landlady let him into Winston's room. *The Wall* wasn't there. Wherever he'd gone, Winston had taken the longest galleys of the decade with him.

Which is probably what caused the secretary who knew him best to start phoning the bars in Winston's neighborhood. He'd once told her that "like writers in Paris," he enjoyed reading and writing "in the local cafés." She phoned the bar on the opposite corner from the stationery store, which Winston had said was his favorite. When the proprietor of the bar said he'd never heard of Winston Atterbury, the two secretaries got the phone book and looked up all the Washington Heights bars and began phoning each in turn. No Winston. Finally, late on Thursday afternoon, one of them phoned the bar on the corner again.

"I told you before, lady, I never heard of the guy!" said the bartender.

"Now don't tell me that!" snapped the secretary, whose nerves were pretty frayed by then. "He lives on your block and we're told he's in your bar regularly."

"I don't know him by name," said the bartender. "If you want to tell me what he looks like, maybe I seen him."

"He's tall, with blond hair and sideburns," said the secretary, "and he dresses —"

"Oh, you mean *Douglas!*" said the bartender. "Just a second. Hey, Douglas! Lady on the phone for you!"

So Winston-alias-Douglas got on the phone and said, Hello, there! How *were* we all? . . . The what? . . . Oh, The *Wall!* Sure, he had it. Had it right there with him. Hadn't got too far into it yet, he'd been busy with his own writing, but it looked to be a pretty fair book, he thought . . .

That was the last we saw of Winston. He moved on to another studio before Monograph had a chance to fire him.

In a business which depended on the Winston Atterburys and

Wide-Margin Wirtzes, the turnover was fairly heavy. Along with whose who were fired, there was the occasional reader who blossomed into a successful writer (Ayn Rand was once an outside reader) and there was the occasional Dolly who didn't need the job and quit when she got bored with it.

We missed Dolly after she left. As I said, she was a sociable, friendly soul and much as we resented her, we all liked her. Jason, who inherited her specialty, mentioned her affectionately one afternoon as he came out of the story editor's office with the new *Ladies' Home Journal.*

"Poor old Dolly," he said, "I wonder if she misses —" And then he stopped cold.

There on the cover of the *Ladies' Home Journal,* streaming across the bottom like a banner, was Dolly's name and the announcement that a story by this gifted new *Journal* writer would be found within.

Dolly'd not only thought she could write better stories than those: she'd gone home and done it.

And I mean to tell you the Monograph Studio outside reading department was fit to be TIED.

·10·

Owl and Piglet on Broadway

ALL I DID was answer a call from Warner Brothers' story department and wander over to Warner's prepared to bootleg a little extra reading — and the sky fell on me.

The state of mind known as "stagestruck" has never been confined to the hopeful young who think they have a creative or performing talent. There are hundreds of men and women who lay no claim to such talents, but who have wangled permanent niches for themselves in the theatre purely because they're incurably stagestruck.

First are the theatrical agents, whose skill at selling and negotiating might have made them richer — and would certainly have given them more security — in any of a dozen mundane industries.

Then there are the backers. They range from the pants manufacturer — whose few thousand dollars invested in a half-million-dollar production gives him the illusion of being In The Theatre — to Howard Cullman, former chairman of the New York Port Authority, who throughout an impressive business career has invested most of his money in Broadway plays.

Third are the theatrical lawyers who take only theatre people as clients, invest their legal fees in their clients' productions and attend preproduction conferences and auditions as assiduously as the producers they wish they were and sometimes become.

In a category all his own was a singular gentleman who died before this book was written, but who is alive and cherished in my memory and will be as long as I live. He is the Owl in this story; and all I knew about him when I wandered over to Warner's that day was that his name was Jacob Wilk and that, publicly, he was the eastern story editor for Warner Brothers Pictures. Privately, Jake Wilk was Broadway's foremost, if not its only, secret producer. This is how he secretly produced plays:

Some reader would cover a novel that seemed a likely vehicle for one of Warner's stars and would recommend the novel to Jake. Jake would read it and decide it would make a fine Broadway play. (Movies didn't interest him.) He'd go over in his mind the names of all Broadway playwrights until he came to the one who was exactly right for this particular book. Then he'd phone the playwright.

"I want you to read this book," he'd say. "I'll send it over to you. I think you ought to adapt it for Broadway."

"I'm tied up right now, Mr. Wilk," the playwright would say with innocent tact, "but as soon as I get time I'll certainly read it."

Jake would send him the book that afternoon and phone the playwright next morning.

"Have you read it yet?" he'd ask.

The playwright in some surprise would repeat that he was "tied up."

"All right," Jake would say agreeably, "I'll be in touch with you."

The next day he'd phone again.

"Have you read it yet?"

He'd keep this up day after day until finally, to get Jake off his back, the playwright would sit down and read the bloody book.

And the next day when Jake phoned, the playwright could say heartily:

"Jake, I've read it and you're right, it would make a very funny play. But I'm all tied up this season. Why don't you get somebody else?"

"That's all right," Jake would say. "I'll wait till you're free."

He'd give the playwright a week and then he'd phone him:

"Are you free yet?"

And from then on he'd phone the playwright every day with "Are you free yet?" until finally the playwright would explode at him over the phone:

"Look, Jake, even if I were free, we don't have the rights to the damn book, we don't have the money and we don't have a producer!" And he'd hang up before Jake could answer.

For a month or so, the playwright would hear nothing further. And just as he'd forgotton all about Jake and his book, Jake would phone him and say:

"We've got the rights to the book, I have a producer and two thirds of the backing, and I can get the final third from Warner's on a preproduction deal as soon as they've seen your script. Are you free yet?"

And so the dazed playwright would sit down and write the play and in due time it would open on Broadway. Some of the plays he secretly produced were smash hits; sometimes, as Jake's daughter put it, there'd be "a string of flops that opened and shut like clams."

But whatever the outcome, from the moment one of his plays went into production, Jake would exhort everybody involved not to mention his name in connection with it. He didn't want Warner's to know he was messing with another Broadway play (though some of Warner's most successful films were made from Jake's Broadway plays).

"Keep my name out of it," he'd say. And they'd keep his name out of it. But they couldn't keep Jake himself out of it. During rehearsals of one of his secret productions he was so incessantly underfoot that the producer and playwright threw him out of the theatre with enough force to break his arm. It didn't stop him. Nothing stopped him. Because when Jake got a Broadway brainstorm it became an obsession. If you thwarted him the obsession intensified.

How I know is, the last of Jake Wilk's obsessions — and the one totally and permanently thwarted by Broadway — was me. You may know what it's like to have an obsession. You've got no idea what it's like to be one.

As I said, it began with a phone call.

"This is Warner Brothers' story department," a secretary said. "Can you stop in and see Mr. Jacob Wilk, our story editor, this afternoon?"

I assumed that Gene Burr, Jake's assistant, had recommended me as a reader. Gene Burr had bought me a drink a few weeks earlier to tell me how much he liked my new play, and he knew I was struggling to make ends meet on Monograph's pittance. I went over to Warner's and up to the story department and was ushered, all unsuspecting, into the office of Mr. Wilk.

He sat behind a cluttered desk, the walls around him covered with framed posters of Broadway hits which I assumed he had purchased for Warner's. He had, but of course that's not why they were on the wall. He'd secretly produced all of them.

He looked up when I entered and glared at me from behind rimless spectacles. He had greying sandy hair and a strong, unremarkable sixty-year-old face.

"Hello," he barked. "Sit down!"

I sat, quaking. I didn't know then that Jake never spoke, he barked, and he never smiled, he glared, and he never had the slightest idea that that's what he did.

On his desk was the familiar blue-bound copy of my play which

Gene Burr had liked and had given him to read, and Jake now glared at that.

"This is a good play," he snapped. "Who's seen it?"

I gave him the names of the four producers who had so far turned it down.

"Who's your agent?" he barked. I told him. He reached for the phone and called my agent and demanded to know who else had seen the play.

"Has Leland seen it?" he rapped into the phone. "Irene?" He listened a moment and said impatiently, "All right. I'll be in touch with you," and hung up. Then he looked past me and bawled out of the open office door like a train conductor:

"Where's Leland Hayward?"

Jake had a secretary and two assistants and he never addressed any one of them by name in my hearing. When he wanted something, he just bawled into empty space and whoever was within earshot came running. This time both the secretary and Gene Burr came running.

"Leland Hayward's in Rome on his honeymooon," said Gene.

"Take a note to him," barked Jake, and as this was clearly meant for the secretary, Gene withdrew. "Dear Leland. Let me know what you think of this script as soon as possible. Regards, Jake." He handed the secretary the blue-bound script and said: "Get his address in Rome. Send it airmail."

It passed through my mind that Leland Hayward might be less than eager to spend his honeymoon reading my play. Such an extraneous thought never passed through Jake Wilk's mind. He glared at me and said:

"Get me some scripts. Irene hasn't seen it, Guthrie hasn't seen it, nobody's seen it!"

Believe me, everybody was going to.

During the next few weeks, the play was airmailed to Leland Hayward on his honeymoon and sent by messenger to Irene Selz-

nick, who was in the hospital recovering from surgery. It went to
Guthrie McClintic and Gilbert Miller and Kermit Bloomgarden
and then on down the line of lesser producers. Within a couple of
months, every producer on Broadway had read it and for assorted
reasons turned it down. Jake spent an afternoon tabulating the
reasons. The next morning my phone rang. When I said hello, a
voice at the other end, like a voice barking the final order to a
firing squad, rapped:

"Wilk!"

I jumped slightly and said how-was-he and Jake said:

"I've found out what's the matter with this play. You'll have to
rewrite it."

"I generally do," I said.

"All right, we'd better have lunch," he snapped. "Sardi's! One
o'clock!"

I walked into Sardi's five minutes early but Jake was there
ahead of me, sitting at a large round table for five at the back of
the room. This was his table. Whether he ate alone or had six
guests, that's where he sat. The two of us lunched with the width
of the table between us, most of the width taken up by letters
from producers telling Jake what was wrong with the play. We
discussed the play's faults, and over coffee we mapped out an
entirely new plot.

(The play's characters and setting appealed to everybody; the
play's plot appealed to nobody. I mention this to keep you from
wondering what was the matter with my plays. That's what was
the matter with all of them. I'd never liked fiction and fiction was
getting back at me: I never could invent a story worth a damn.)

The coffee came in a silver pot and as we talked, Jake tapped
the pot absently with a finger to see if it was hot — then with two
fingers, then three. As soon as he could press four fingers against it
without pain, he bawled at any waiter going past:

"Coffee's not hot!"

and the waiter carried off the old pot and brought a fresh one. During our two-hour conference we ran through four pots.

(What paralyzes me about this finger-tapping procedure is that Jake bequeathed it to me. Sitting over my breakfast or dinner coffee to this day, I tap the pot to see if it's hot. Thanks to a long association with Jake Wilk, if the coffee's not scalding I can't drink it.)

When we left Sardi's, he asked how long I thought the revisions would take and I said I hoped to do them in six weeks.

"Fine," he said. "I'll be in touch with you."

I started work on the revisions at nine o'clock the next morning. At ten o'clock the phone rang.

"Wilk!" barked the firing squad. "How's it coming?"

I thought How - the - hell - do - you - think - it's - coming - I - only - started-an-hour-ago. I said it was coming fine.

"Good," said Jake. "I'll be in touch with you."

Next morning at ten he phoned again. He phoned the morning after that and the morning following. He phoned every day for a month, as regularly as he brushed his teeth, and the conversation never varied.

"Wilk! How's it coming?"

"Fine."

"Good. I'll be in touch with you."

At the beginning of the sixth week, the password changed. When the phone rang at ten and I said hello, he didn't ask how it was coming, he didn't even rap "Wilk!" He just barked:

"Well, where is it?"

And for the rest of the week it was Where is it? which drove me on Friday to promise him I'd finish it over the weekend. That Saturday, in the dirty apartment I normally cleaned on Saturday, I typed from 9 A.M. to midnight, breaking my back to meet Jake Wilk's mythical deadline. I crawled beaten into bed at 1 A.M., slept late on Sunday and was nearly halfway through breakfast before he called and said Where was it?

"I still have the last scene to type, and then I have to separate the carbons and bind the copies," I said. "I'll drop it at your office tomorrow."

"I'll be home tonight," he said. "Drop it off here with the doorman. I'll read it before I go to bed."

I worked all day Sunday. I finished binding one copy of the script at six o'clock, and without stopping to wash my face I tore out of the house (Maudiebird's little hovel on Ninety-fifth Street) and down to Sixty-eighth Street to the plush Fifth Avenue apartment house where Jake lived, and left the script with the doorman. Then I went home and collapsed. Lying on the studio couch staring up at the ceiling, I lectured myself bitterly.

"Why," I asked myself, "are you ruining your health for this madman? He could have waited till tomorrow. He could have waited till Adelaide's wedding day in *Guys and Dolls*, which if I remember was the Twelfth of Never!"

Joy came in the morning: no phone call. It was the producers' turn for a while.

None of the producers who read the new version wanted any part of it. (If you can't invent plots you can't invent plots.) But, as I said, Jake Wilk's obsession was not that particular play, it was me. During the weeks I had worked on the revisions, he had read his readers' reports on several of my old plays and he now wanted to read the plays for himself. I'd thrown away most of them but there were two I'd kept and I sent them to him. He liked both of them. And having failed to get my Play No. 14 produced, he now went to work on Nos. 9 and 11.

For a solid winter, he tried to sell them. Not until he had exhausted — and I mean exhausted — the last producer and backer on Broadway did he admit defeat.

He sat in his office with me at twilight of a March afternoon, holding in his hands the last script which had just come back from the last possible producer. He put the script down and stared at it. Then his eyes moved to No. 14, which was his favorite and which it seemed to me was always on his desk. He picked it up in both hands and hefted it gently.

"Just can't crack the ice," he muttered. It was the first time I ever heard him sound tired. "So much talent, it's all here . . ." And he barked fiercely again: "We just have to crack the ice!"

I wanted to speak and I couldn't. He was an eminently success- ful man with a massive list of achievements, both public and *sub rosa*, and there he sat, glaring at No. 14 and mumbling tiredly again: ". . . just can't crack the ice . . ." I wanted to comfort him for my failure to write a good play. But of course, to Jake it wasn't my failure at all, it was Broadway's failure. Broadway was blind, and with all his driving force he couldn't make Broadway see.

It took him a month to bounce back. It was actually a pleasure, when the phone rang one April morning, to hear "Wilk!" barked at me from the other end.

"Have you got an idea for a new play yet?" he asked.

"No," I said. "I wish I had."

"What do you do all day besides read for Monograph?" he demanded. I could have said, "I'm trying to memorize my Greek middle voice endings" but I didn't.

"Nothing much," I said.

"You don't get ideas sitting around waiting for them," he said. "I'll find you some work to do. Then you'll get an idea. All right, I'll be in touch with you."

A few days later he phoned back.

"I have a very talented boy here," he announced. "He's a song- writer. He has a musical he wants the studios to buy but the book's not very good. He doesn't want to submit the book, he needs a good presentation. You want to write him a presentation? He'll pay you for it."

I said I'd love to.

"Sardi's!" snapped Jake. "One o'clock!"

He was there ahead of me again. When I threaded my way to his back table he was already sitting at it.

Sitting next to him, talking nonstop in a joyous bellow, was the "very talented boy," a round, beaming Mr. Five-by-Five who had written the lyrics to *No, No, Nanette* thirty years earlier.

"This is Irving Caesar," rapped Jake. "He's a very talented boy."

"How do you do," I said.

"Hello, dolling!" Irving bellowed, beaming.

They were insane opposites. Where Jake was lean and unsmiling, Irving was completely round and had a beaming smile which never left his face for an instant. Where Jake said little and barked it, Irving talked continuously and hollered it. But who wants to sit at the quietest table in Sardi's?

A "presentation" was a long synopsis written as a press agent or the show's producer might write it, the object being to persuade the studio that the script was sensational. If you had to redesign the plot, misrepresent some characters and add or delete a few, nobody minded — least of all the studio, which, if it bought the script, would turn it over to five or six new writers anyway.

But the musical comedy Irving wanted a presentation of was called *My Dear Public*. It had been a flop on Broadway, and a bore to me when I'd read it for Monograph. I thought it only fair to tell Irving this.

"What the hell, dolling, you'll make it look sensational!" he beamed, and I was hired.

I did an outline of the presentation and mailed it to Irving for his approval. He phoned me as soon as he read it.

"Dolling, you're a genius, I don't know how you do it!" he said. "I'll buy you a steak at Gallagher's to celebrate. Nine o'clock, can you wait to eat till nine o'clock? I can't stand to eat early, the waiters got no time to pay attention. Nine o'clock, all right, dolling?"

So we met for dinner at Gallagher's Steak House at nine o'clock.

"Bring her a thick one!" Irving bellowed, beaming at the waiter. "She's my genius, she lives in a tenement!" He hadn't seen my apartment but he'd seen the address on the envelope I mailed him. Tenement.

While we waited for the steaks, Irving told me about himself. In addition to *No, No, Nanette* he'd written the lyrics to "Swanee" way back when, he wrote musical scores for the Ringling Brothers' Circus and he'd written a couple of hundred Safety Songs and Friendship Songs for schoolchildren across the country. The Friendship Songs, he told me, had been translated into ten languages. He was a member of the board of ASCAP and an occasional Broadway producer. He was currently at work on songs for a new musical to be called *Kisses and Knishes,* and he would sing me the score as soon as it was finished.

"I'm a bachelor," he told me as the steaks came, beaming benevolently at mine when he saw it was thick enough, and benevolently at the sliced cucumbers and tomatoes when he saw they were thick enough because usually they were too thin. "Marriage is all right, I got nothing against it, but why should I restrict myself to one woman? But so all right, so that's how I am, so I got this suite at the Park Central — Lissen, whaddaya think it costs me every morning to get *The New York Times?* A dollar ninety-five. Because how can you phone down every morning and say, 'Send me up a *New York Times*'? You can't, you gotta phone down and order breakfast, I don't eat breakfast but every day I phone down and order breakfast and then I say casually" — he tossed his head and waved a fat arm airily to show me how casually he did it — " 'Oh, by the way, send me up a *New York Times.*' The breakfast is a dollar fifty-five, you gotta tip the kid and pay him for *The Times* so *The New York Times* costs me a dollar ninety-five every day. I should write and tell them that. Should I?"

At which moment, the headwaiter came over to our table.

"Irving, how's the steak?" he asked.

When I said that Irving's face never lost its beaming smile I meant that he not only beamed happily, he could also beam sadly. He now beamed very sadly at the waiter and said:

"I wish I could say it was great! I wish I could!" And he shook his head, still beaming sadly.

"How's the lady's steak?" the waiter asked me.

"What're you asking *her?*" Irving beamed with a snort attached. "What would *she* know, she's a starving writer, she lives in a tenement, where would she get a steak unless I buy it for her? To her it tastes good!"

And don't think it didn't.

After dinner, he put me in a cab, paid the driver and said, "Sweet dreams, dolling, I'll call you," before departing off down Broadway in a round, rolling, eager gait that would have done both Milne and Piglet proud.

Irving was — and I hope still is — the happiest man I ever knew. He loved everybody and everything, but most especially he loved Broadway — where he lived, ate, worked and spent his evenings-out. He loved all of it, from the marquees and big neon signs to the honky-tonk gift shops and shooting galleries. Broadway was his ocean and he bounced around on top of it like a cork, on intimate terms with every wave, every piece of seaweed and every shark. ("Frank's a very nice fella!" he told me earnestly, speaking of the notorious gangster Frank Costello. "He gives big to the Heart Fund!")

He called me one day, when I'd nearly finished the presentation, and told me to meet him for lunch at Dinty Moore's and he'd sing me the score of *Kisses and Knishes*. But he didn't sing it to me at Dinty Moore's. He waited, and sang the score to me as we walked down Broadway afterward, he on his way to his office and I on my way to Monograph.

Walking down Broadway on a spring afternoon with Irving Caesar singing to you at the top of his stentorian lungs is what they call an Experience.

He'd finish a chorus of a song, and I'd say:

"That's a very pretty —"

"NOW WAIT!" he'd holler, seizing my arm to halt me in my tracks in case I wasn't planning to wait, and keeping a firm grip on me as he sang the second verse and another round of the chorus. Then he'd let my arm go and we'd walk on a few more steps while he set the scene for the next song for me.

People were going by in a steady stream as we walked, and at every step we took, somebody coming along would wave or tip his hat or nod, and say, "Hello, Irving" or "Hi, Irving," or "Hiya, Mr. Caesar." Everybody who went by seemed to know him: cops and song pluggers, actors and fight promoters and prostitutes, bookies and Broadway producers and winos and panhandlers. Everybody spoke to him and Irving beamed back and waved and said How-ya-doin'? and Call-me-I'll-buya-a-drink, and never lost a beat of the song he was singing from *Kisses and Knishes*.

I finished the presentation and Irving pronounced it magnificent and predicted we'd both get rich on the sale of *My Dear Public* to some movie studio. He hurried off to sell it and I took a week to pick up my scattered wits and straighten them out.

He phoned a few weeks later to tell me that all the studios had rejected *My Dear Public*. I said I was sorry.

"Don't worry about it! Forget it!" Irving advised me on the phone, his tone of voice as enthusiastic as if he'd just made a million dollars on the sale. "It didn't work, that's yesterday! Forget it, I forgot it already! I got a million projects, get yourself a project, dolling! Write a play, I'll put money in it.' "

"It's funny you should say that," I told him, "because just this morning, for the first time in a year, I got an idea for one."

"See, dolling?" he said triumphantly. "So who needs the presentation? Write a funny play, I'll put money in it."

That was on a Friday. The new play wouldn't take form enough for me to start writing for several weeks and it would be one more unproducible dog when I did write it. But if you're a writer and you've got an idea for something solid to write, you're happy as Christmas morning. On Saturday night, therefore, I stayed out late, celebrating. One of the male readers at Monograph bought us a lavish pair of standing-room tickets to a Broadway musical and we went on to a party afterward. When I finally crawled into bed shortly before dawn it was with the secure knowledge that I could sleep till noon on Sunday.

And I would have, if the phone hadn't wakened me at ten. Without opening my eyes I sent an exploratory arm out toward the night table, located the phone and pulled the receiver onto my pillow. Still with my eyes closed I mumbled:

"Hello?"

"Wilk!" snapped my guardian angel at the other end. "Irving says you have a new play. How's it coming?"

· 11 ·

"Lhude Sing Cuccu"

"I've had summer theatres," I said to Maxine one spring day in the early fifties. "I'm going to apply to the MacDowell Colony this year instead."

"The what?" said Maxine.

"It's an artists' colony," I said.

She threw me a dubious look.

"What's it like?" she asked.

"Now how would I know?" I said. "Ask me when I come home."

When I wrote to the Colony's New York office for an application blank, all I knew about the place was what I'd read in magazine articles: that it was in the pine woods of New Hampshire and had been founded (in 1906) by Mrs. Edward MacDowell, widow of the American composer. She had built it as a haven where composers, painters and writers could come for a few summer weeks, to work in absolute peace, free of the pressures of having to earn a living.

The application blank arrived in the mail, along with a glossy brochure containing photos of a few of the twenty-five studios. You could apply for a studio for one of three six-week periods between May and September. On the application blank, you had to list your "Creative Achievements" and describe the work you wanted to do at the Colony. (I-won-a-fellowship-once, I-was-a-Theatre-Guild-protégée, I-have-a-play-under-option-and-the-producer-wants-it-rewritten.) You had to enclose with your application two letters of recommendation from "Persons Eminent in Your Profession" and I got Terry Helburn and Jake Wilk to write glowing testimonials for me.

On the day the letter came telling me I'd been accepted, I wished I hadn't applied. In spite of the brochure's description of happy working days in solitary studios and long, cozy evenings with your fellow-artists, I set out nervously for Peterborough, New Hampshire, with a mammoth suitcase, my portable typewriter and no idea what to expect. (Unless you count my gloomy conviction that I was going to be surrounded for six weeks by Genuine Creative Artists who would look down on me.)

I reached the Colony in time for dinner. And the odd thing was that even when I'd been there an evening and had seen all the main buildings, I still didn't know what to expect.

The main buildings were clustered together in a clearing in a six-hundred-acre pine forest. The chief building, Colony Hall, was a large white clapboard house with a big, old-fashioned living room, a dining room with half a dozen tables each seating four or five and a big kitchen where they locked up everything at night. (How I found this out is, five of us got hungry one midnight and spent half an hour ransacking kitchen cabinets looking for anything edible that wasn't locked away in high cupboards. Nothing.)

Next to Colony Hall was an old rambling frame house where the women slept, next to that was the library and way off down the road out of sight was the Men's Lodge where the men slept, built good and far from the women's building to discourage That Sort of Thing. (Mrs. MacDowell had overseen the construction of the buildings in 1906.)

Those buildings were all I saw of the Colony that evening, and all tourists ever see of it. You learn what the Colony is like on your first day — and from then on all days are miraculously the same.

If you're an early riser you're up and dressed in a bathing suit with heavy wool sweater and pants over it at 7:30 A.M., when a teenaged waitress comes out of Colony Hall, stations herself on the lawn and clangs a cowbell enthusiastically. First call to breakfast.

You race over to the dining room and join the other early risers. There are only five or six colonists up that early and you all squeeze together at one table, known as the Early Table and so famous for its high good humor that now and then a late-riser would stagger into the dining room in time for the conversation at the Early Table and then go back to bed.

You eat an enormous breakfast. (This is particularly true of the men, for reasons which will become apparent at lunchtime. From a masculine point of view, lunch at the MacDowell Colony simply passes belief.) At 8:45, you bid a reluctant farewell to human society and go down to your studio. If you can find it.

You enter the surrounding pine forest by one of four main roads leading to the studios. But the studios have been scattered so far apart through the six-hundred-acre woods that the painter in one studio can hear neither the piano to his east nor the typewriter to his west. So each main studio road has several forks, each branching into a narrow dirt path leading to a single studio. The problem, as you trudge down your main studio road, is to remember whether you take the second fork to your northeast or the third fork southwest, always providing you know which way is north, which I personally don't.

And since the cardinal Colony rule is that no one may enter anyone else's studio at any time without invitation, you cannot stop in at the Omicron, say, if you happen to arrive there by mistake, and ask the composer inside if he knows where the Veltin is. Instead, you go back to Colony Hall — if you can find *that* — and say to the manager:

"Cousin, I've lost it again."

And the manager takes you down to your studio in the Colony truck.

You're probably wondering how a studio came to be called the Omicron. Any patron generous enough to donate a studio to the Colony may name it anything he, she or it likes. (Omicron was donated by some sorority, I think. I've no idea who, or what, Veltin was.) The patron is also entitled to build it any way he, she or it likes, so the studios run a gamut in nomenclature from the Alexander to the Monday Music, and in architecture from Italian Palazzo to Backwoods Monastic. Whatever its style, each studio seems to have one demented feature all its own.

Take my favorite studio, the Veltin, which is the one I had that first summer. It's a perfect example of Backwoods Monastic architecture: a plain wooden shack with a bare wooden floor, bare wooden work tables, two straight chairs, an old rocker and a big fireplace. Out back on the porch is what in Thomas Jefferson's day was called a Necessary and that's about all that can be said for it.

Well, in the middle of the floor of this bare hut is a glossy, white-enameled staircase complete with newel posts, its five or six steps leading up to a landing, big enough for you to stand on with your head just clearing the ceiling (if you're short). After you've stood there awhile you come back down because there's nowhere else to go. The steps don't go anywhere. Over lunch I used to speculate endlessly on what the architect had in mind.

But whether you're writing in the Veltin or painting in the Alexander (a replica of a seventeenth-century Swiss chapel, reproduced stone for stone and stained-glass window for stained-glass window), once you've walked in and shut the door, all studios are magically alike. All your life you've worked in dark rooms above noisy streets, with the phone ringing, the radio overhead blaring, the baby next door crying. Here in your studio you will work, for the first time, in absolute quiet and inviolable privacy through a long uninterrupted day. And you offer up a prayer for the soul of Mrs. Edward MacDowell, who gave it to you.

As soon as you come in in the morning, you build a fire in your fireplace. Then you either nod to your tombstone or studiously avoid it. Your tombstone stands on the mantel over the fireplace. It's a wooden plaque shaped like an old-fashioned headstone, on which you'll find the signature of every colonist who worked in that studio before you. If your tombstone has a line reading:

Thornton Wilder — Playwright — 1937

which tells you that Thornton Wilder wrote *Our Town* sitting where you're getting ready to sit, it can put you off your aim — till you notice that his name is followed by a long list of writers you never heard of, which makes you feel better.

Having made the fire, you sharpen your pencils, clean your typewriter, stack your typing paper neatly and put your cigarettes and ashtray within reach. Then you stare out the window at the trees. And then, having completely run out of dodges, you get to work. By one o'clock you've finished two days' work. The sun is high and hot and you've let the fire go out and peeled down to your bathing suit. You go out to the back porch and splash your face and wash your hands and discover you're so hungry you could eat anything. And you're about to.

You go out to the front step of your studio and take in the wicker basket which has been left there for you. You clear off a work table and take out of the lunch basket and arrange on the table: three little cellophane bags, four sealed paper cups, two thermos bottles, two plastic-wrapped sandwiches — one of which is known to colonists as "the Other sandwich" — and a rolled-up paper napkin containing cutlery. Bouncing around by itself at the bottom of the basket is probably an apple. For later.

Cellophane bag No. 1 contains a carrot, a scallion, a radish and a stick of celery. This is salad. Bag No. 2 has whole-wheat crackers to eat with your soup, which is in thermos No. 1. Bag No.

3 is sugar for the coffee in thermos No. 2. Paper cup No. 1 contains half a stewed peach. This is not dessert, this is compote. How you know is, paper cup No. 3 has the dessert: last night's cake doused with sauce (which is why they locked up last night's cake after dinner). Paper cup No. 2 is mayonnaise for sandwich No. 1. Paper cup No. 4 is cream for the coffee.

One sandwich contains meat. The Other sandwich may contain absolutely anything. Whatever's in it is smooth, soft, a pretty color and hard to identify. You taste it, you smell it, you carry it to the window and peer closely at it — and still, you eat it without the slightest idea of what you're eating. When you get back up to Colony Hall that night, you ask the cook what you ate. One, for instance, was a bright pale mauve and turned out to be cream cheese and apple butter beaten up together. Another was just plain mashed figs.

("They ask you," a young composer said to me earnestly at dinner that night, "to write down on your basket all the things you don't like. I wrote 'liverwurst and sardines.' Who thinks to put down 'I don't like mashed fig sandwiches'?")

After lunch guilt drives you back to the typewriter and you work till five or five-thirty, when you quit and survey the shambles. The floor is strewn with fireplace ashes and balled-up paper discards, your apple and one shoe are on the mantel, your sweater's on the newel post, your pants are on the landing and you can't find your other shoe. (It's out back by the Necessary.) You're hot, tired and dirty, but you burn the trash, sweep the floor and fireplace and stack the finished pages of your manuscript neatly before trudging back up to Colony Hall to shower and dress before the dinner cowbell.

At dinner you meet your fellow-artists. Five or six, at least, are college professors — who, with their steady salaries, their tenure, their sabbaticals, Fulbrights and pension plans, are the Colony's filthy rich. The rest are full-time working artists with an uncertain income and half the time no income at all.

For the first few evenings you're so mellowed by your utopian days you love everybody. After that, you find the four or five colonists most congenial to you and you spend your evenings with them — especially when, as happens at least once a week, the evening begins with a cultural crisis precipitated at dinner.

Either Wanda, a wispy poetess, taps her water glass for attention during dessert, and announces that on Tuesday evening the Colony poets will give a Reading of their poems in Colony Hall for their fellow-colonists; or Alfred, a painter, announces that he will give a lecture on Nonrepresentational Trends in the library on Friday evening and he's going to serve sherry afterward (if the kitchen lets him have the glasses). Or Professor Kimmel, composer, aged seventy-two, lets it be known through a disciple that he can be prevailed upon to play a recording of his twelve-tone symphony this evening and his studio is large enough to accommodate everybody.

When one of these gruesome offerings is advertised, you go off after dinner to huddle under a tree with your gang and have a heated argument about whether you *have* to go to this thing or not. (*Pro:* "We can't insult our fellow-artists! Everybody's sensitive, we can't hurt Wanda's feelings." *Con:* "I worked hard all day, I'm damned if I'm going to spend the evening listening to Alfred run off at the mouth for two hours!" Or more simply: "I had Alfred for dinner; that's enough.") When two of these entertainments were advertised for two different evenings of the same week, we compromised: we went to the Poetry Reading on Tuesday; and on Friday, the night of Nonrepresentational Trends, we snuck off to Peterborough to see Joel McCrea in a horse opera. Alfred wasn't speaking to us on Saturday, of course, but he got over it.

You're there for six weeks, and for five of them you're blissfully happy. And then abruptly, early in the sixth week, you become violently sick of the place and you want to go home. It happens without warning when the Colony's one zombie — in dyed orange beard and purple shorts — praises Ezra Pound's political views once too often, or a mousy woman you're fond of turns out to be a solitary drinker. Or a letter from home may do it.

It happened to me when I came up from the studio one hazy afternoon to find a thick letter waiting for me, addressed in Maxine's lavish, all-over-the-envelope handwriting. It was postmarked Washington, D.C., and written on Hotel Willard stationery, several pages of it, and after I bathed and dressed I parked myself under a tree to read it before dinner.

"I just want you to know," wrote Maxine, "that while you've been rubbing noses with the Intelligentsia, I have been making my singing debut. Of course, they only let me sing on opening night and I am a *little* put out about that.

"I got back from the Cape on a Sunday night and there was a message to call Eddie at home the minute I got in. He'd left his home phone number — and when an agent wants you to call him at home on a Sunday night, you *must* be right for the part.

"I called him and he said a new show was getting ready to try out in Washington, they needed a last-minute replacement for the ingenue, and I should fly down to Washington Monday morning. I flew down and gave my usual superb audition and Bobby, the director, said: 'Fine, dear. We open Friday, take the script home and study it and come back after lunch and we'll get to work.'

"So I got a hotel room and locked myself in with the script and read the first act where I didn't have much to do, and then I read the second act where I had a big scene, and in the middle of the big scene it said in the script: '*She drapes herself over the piano and sings.*' Sings? Maxine Stuart sings??

"So when I went to the theatre I said to Bobby: 'Lissen, I think you better hear me sing,' and he said: 'Sure, baby, I want to, now let's get to work.' And we rehearsed the first act. On Tuesday morning we started the second act, and we got to where I was supposed to drape myself over the piano and sing 'He Ain't Got

· 142 ·

Rhythm' and Bobby called out: 'We'll get you the sheet music later. Skip the song for now.'

"Wednesday they gave me the sheet music which I couldn't read. On my dinner hour I went around to a music store and played a record of 'He Ain't Got Rhythm' and learned the tune in my fashion. But on Thursday, when dress rehearsal started, I still hadn't sung for anybody so I went over to Bobby and said: 'Lissen, I think you better hear me sing,' and he said: 'Just speak the words today; save your voice for the opening.'

"On opening night, Don, who plays the piano in the scene, stopped by my dressing room and said: 'How did the key sound to you? Can you manage that A all right?' And I said: 'Well, I can certainly try!' I felt so educated, knowing there was an A in it.

"The first act went by like a breeze, and in the second act I made my entrance in my black-lace-over-pink-net-with-flounce evening gown and on cue, Don started to play and I draped myself over the top of the piano and began to sing 'He Ain't Got Rhythm' in my one note. I sang about four bars — making a great important message out of the words so nobody'd notice there wasn't much tune — when I heard the piano getting very loud. I pushed my resonance all the way up and gave it my full projection and I still couldn't top the piano. And I thought: 'That scene-hog has *got* to be made to take his foot off the pedal. Nobody can hear me.' Well, I finished triumphantly — by which I mean the note I finished on was very close to the note the piano finished on — and I said to myself: 'You see? There's nothing to it.'

"After the show, we were all standing around on stage waiting for the management's criticisms and cuts and so forth, and Bobby came over and put his arm around me and said: 'Maxine, honey, you're great in the part, now-lemme-ask-you-something. How are you at pantomime?' So of course I said I was great at that, too, and Bobby said: 'Fine, baby, fine, now why don't we get a record of some blues singer singing "He Ain't Got Rhythm" and you can just drape over the piano and pantomime the words and you won't have to bother singing.'

"The show got appalling notices so it's closing after Washington, and I'll be home in two weeks. Trust you'll be the same. Arty studios in New England are all very well for the summer but it'll be coming on Fall soon and you should be just *panting* to get back to the big wide world of unemployment and telephones and trucks clanking down Second Avenue."

And just as suddenly as that, I was panting to get back to it.

·12·

A Round Trip through the Annex
or
Sarah Wants to Do Something
Greek and Other Stories

ON A SPRING DAY in 1952, a worried young dentist named Joey
lifted his melting brown eyes from my X rays to me and said
sadly:

"It's staggering. There's no room left for any more fillings."
Like George Washington, I had bad teeth.

I was faced, he said, with a choice: I could have all my teeth
capped, for roughly $2,500; or I could have all my teeth out and
replaced with false ones, for roughly $2,500.

Since I was earning $50 a week at Monograph and had $92 in
the bank, I went home and suggested to the Lord that this was an
ideal moment for a miracle. What I had in mind, of course, was
that if He really felt like it, the Lord could get one of my plays
produced on Broadway and have it run long enough to make me
$2,500. What the Lord had in mind, of course, was Flanagan's
Law.

Literally ten minutes after I discussed miracles with my Crea-
tor, the telephone rang and Gene Burr said Hi, how was I, and I
said Fine, where was he? I knew he'd left Jake Wilk's office at
Warner's but I didn't know where he'd gone.

"That's what I'm calling about," said Gene. "How would you like to write for television?"

Television was barely four years old and I knew nothing whatever about it. Before I could say this, Gene added carelessly: "It's only two bills."

"Two what?" I asked.

"Two hundred dollars for a half-hour script."

Two hundred dollars would buy two porcelain tooth-jackets. If I wrote a script a month for a year, Joey could live on the television money and I could live on the Monograph money.

"You're sent from Heaven," I told Gene Burr. "What show is it?"

"The Adventures of Ellery Queen," he said. "It's a low-budget show on a little network called DuMont. I'm the story editor. Come on down to my office tomorrow afternoon and we'll talk."

The next afternoon, driven every inch of the way by the simple desire to have teeth, I became a writer of television murders.

A few weeks later, Maxine dropped in one morning for a cup of coffee. After two seasons of unemployment she was grimly pleased to report that she was working at last. She could be seen nightly, she informed me, on all the better TV channels.

"What show are you in?" I asked.

"I am not in a show. I do a solo act," said Maxine acidly. "I am the Blue Cheer girl." Blue Cheer, she explained to me, was a detergent. She was selling it on television.

This is not just how Maxine and I got into television in the fifties, it's how everybody got into television in the fifties. Unable to get rid of us any other way, the theatre had built an Annex and flogged us into it.

(Gene Burr, who had wanted to be a Broadway producer and whose Ellery Queen writers were all failed playwrights, put it more brutally but defined it for all of us with deadly precision. "Television," he said, "is the asshole of the theatre.")

The budget for Ellery Queen was so small that the cast of each script was limited to five characters. Since two of them had to be Ellery and his father, it left you only three characters for the murder plot: the character who got murdered (known as the corpse) and two suspects, one innocent and one guilty. But in addition to the five full parts, we were allowed two "five-liners" — actors who, for the pittance they were paid, were permitted by Actors' Equity to speak five lines and no more. These five-liners were very useful to the writer; you kept them standing around looking silent and villainous.

I myself brought a unique extra dimension to Ellery's adventures. Until I came on the scene, the show's scripts had been evenly divided between low-brow and middle-brow murders. In prizefight and racetrack murders, the suspects and corpses spoke uneducated English and were therefore low-brow, while murders involving politicians or businessmen were middle-brow. What the show lacked was a group of distinctly high-brow murders in which the suspects and corpses were all cultured. That was my contribution. I became Ellery Queen's special writer of arty murders. I wrote six: murder in the art gallery, murder at the opera, murder in the concert hall, murder at the Shakespeare festival and two murders at the ballet. And we were just getting round to the rare-book business when the show went off the air.

Nobody outside the industry would have believed the physical restrictions of live television. Ellery Queen was televised in a large rehearsal hall, a bare room blocked off into the three separate stage sets which were all the budget allowed. Well, in "Murder at the Opera," if Ellery played one scene in an opera star's dressing room and the next scene in his own living room, you couldn't give him the last few lines in the dressing-room scene or the first few lines in the living-room scene because he needed ten seconds off-camera to walk from the dressing-room set to the living-room set. And if he wore white tie and tails in the opera scene, you put him in his living room in the next scene, so that during his ten-second walk he could slip a long dressing gown over his evening clothes. I mean, you didn't take him from the opera scene and put him on a beach in the next scene because there was never time for costume changes, there was only time to slip one costume over another.

But the technical restrictions were easy to learn. What made writing this nonsense the hardest work I'd ever done was the appalling economy imposed by the clock and the small budget. Out of five characters and two five-liners, you had to create the illusion of an entire opera company or a full symphony orchestra. And the economy of background was nothing compared with the economy of words demanded by the clock, which ordered you to tell a complete story in twenty-six minutes. You were constantly forced to compress eight or ten rambling lines of dialogue into one succinct one — to say nothing of having to create a believable character in five lines.

The result was that in a year of grinding out shabby murder stories of which I was ashamed, I learned more about dramatic writing than Aristotle, Stanislavski and Terry Helburn had ever been able to teach me. This didn't infuriate me at the time because I didn't know it. All I knew was that to avoid being toothless, I had sunk to the depths of literary depravity.

This view oppressed me less when I graduated from Ellery Queen to more respectable dramatic shows. But then as now, American television was controlled by the large corporations who "sponsored" — paid for — every show, and not only interrupted each play several times to sell soap or cars or underarm deodorants, but also dictated what the writer might, and might not, say in a script. Because of this — and in spite of the fact that I enjoyed writing TV scripts — I never overcame my conviction that writing for commercial television was a kind of prostitution.

How I know this is that between 1952 and 1959 I must have

written at least fifty television scripts, but through those years I steadily refused to buy a TV set, and I never saw a single show I wrote.

Maxine insisted that the Annex had no such traumatic effect on her, but I maintain that anyone who could send the Blue Cheer ad agency executive the Christmas present Maxine sent was expressing an obvious death wish. Maxine insisted she wasn't jeopardizing her job because her career as the Blue Cheer girl was doomed anyway.

Blue Cheer detergent came in fine powdery crystals in a blue box. The way the commercial was written, Maxine was supposed to hold out her cupped hands while some unseen spirit poured Blue Cheer into them from a mammoth box overhead. Then the camera moved in for a close-up of Maxine's cupped hands full of Blue Cheer while she rattled away about the fine quality of the granules. But Maxine turned out to have peculiar fingers. No matter how tightly she cupped her hands, there was a narrow space between all of her fingers. So while she was enthusiastically describing the fine granules, the said granules were sifting through her fingers in a messy cloud which spilled all over the floor and loused up the whole commercial.

Well, the hell with it, the Blue Cheer people must have said to themselves, because they rewrote the script so that all Maxine had to do was hold a big box of Blue Cheer in both hands while she talked about the product. She did this so well that after the filming, five Blue Cheer ad agency and company executives converged on her with congratulations.

"Wonderful!" one of them exclaimed. "You held the box absolutely straight!"

Carried away by this praise, Maxine informed me one day that she was shopping for a Christmas gift for the account executive.

"It's done," she assured me blandly. "I've asked around and I'm told you *always* give the account executive a Christmas present."

It took her two weeks to find the right gift and she phoned to tell me about it.

"I sent him a red-and-white Blab-Off," she said. "They come in all colors. I sent him the prettiest."

"What," I inquired, "is a Blab-Off?"

"It's a little gadget you hook onto your TV set," said Maxine. "It has a sign on it that says STOP THOSE ANNOYING TV COMMERCIALS. As soon as a commercial comes on, you push the button on your Blab-Off and the set goes dead for two minutes."

Like me, Maxine later graduated to dramatic shows and, like me, she got over the Shame of it. She has since spent most of her life acting on television and enjoying it thoroughly. And as I said, I had a very good time myself in the Annex, despite a few incidents that might be described as unsettling. The first of these happened on The Hallmark Hall of Fame.

This was in 1953, after the demise of Ellery Queen. I was having lunch with another Monograph reader when I happened to see Ethel Frank, an old acquaintance, having lunch at a nearby table. When she learned I'd been writing for television, she said:

"I'm story editor on The Hallmark Hall of Fame. You ought to write for us. It's a historical show and you like history. Call me tonight and I'll tell you what kind of outline to submit."

I called her for instructions and then submitted an outline on the love story of John Donne. Ethel bought the outline, Albert McCleery, the Hallmark producer, liked the finished script and from then on I was one of seven or eight writers who wrote steadily for the show.

The Hallmark Hall of Fame dramatized incidents in the lives of great men and women. We could select our subjects from any country, any century, any area of greatness, ranging theoretically from Cleopatra to Dickens, from Boadicea to Gershwin. We were restricted only by the taboos imposed on us by the peculiar morality of television in the fifties.

I say "peculiar" because you'll have gathered from Ellery Queen that murder was never considered immoral by American television. Murder was pure entertainment as long as the murderer went to prison or died in the end. The only immorality — the only Sin — was Sex. Every sponsor kept a hawk eye out for any suggestion of this sin in his writers' scripts. And on the outside chance that something sinful might slip past the sponsor's eye, every network maintained its own censorship office to which a copy of every television script had to be submitted.

Well, Hallmark was a biographical show — and you just wouldn't believe how many of the world's great heroes and heroines failed to live up to the moral standards of American television. Boadicea might have got by, but you couldn't possibly write a script about Cleopatra, Dickens or Gershwin without cleaning up their sex lives first.

Plus which, Mr. Joyce C. Hall, owner of the Hallmark Greeting Card Company, sponsor of The Hallmark Hall of Fame, imposed two fascinating taboos of his own. Mr. Hall, whose home and headquarters were in Kansas City, Missouri, was a gentleman of the Old South. Which meant that while we could dramatize the love story of Jefferson Davis, we were forbidden to write scripts about Abraham Lincoln. Or Harriet Beecher Stowe or General Grant or Walt Whitman-who-was-immoral-anyway.

Mr. Hall's second taboo was in deference to the star of The Hallmark Hall of Fame. I've often wondered if she knew about it; I have a feeling it amused her vastly if she did. The mistress of ceremonies on The Hallmark Hall of Fame, and the star of one weekly show in every four, was Sarah Churchill. And Mr. Hall forbade all scripts dealing with heroes of the American Revolution because he wouldn't insult the British Prime Minister's daughter by suggesting the British had lost it.

We submitted our Hallmark outlines on special paper with a printed legend across the top:

We nominate . . . . for
The Hallmark Hall of Fame *because:*

. . . .

. . . .

After "nominate" you filled in the name of the great man or woman; after "*because*" you stated his-or-her chief claim to fame. On the rest of the page you outlined the particular incident or event in the nominee's life which you wanted to dramatize.

But in actual practice, "We nominate . . . *because*" was likely to mean a phone call from Ethel Frank:

"Listen, we need something for the Jewish holidays, you want to do Joseph and his coat-of-many-colors or some damn thing?"

Or:

"Hon, dig up somebody for Sarah for Valentine's Day and call me back on it, will you?"

Since Sarah starred in one show a month we were constantly beating the bushes for heroines she could play. So it was a help when Sarah herself came up with a suggestion, which one day she did.

Though all the scripts were written in New York, the Hallmark show was produced in Hollywood and there were daily transcontinental phone calls between Ethel in New York and Albert McCleery in Hollywood. It was after one such phone call that Ethel phoned me.

"Sarah," she announced, "wants to do something Greek."

Greek?

"Ethel," I said, "except for an occasional queen who murdered her family, Greek women did not go out and get famous. Of course," I added tentatively, "there's Sappho."

"Sappho's out," said Ethel. "Mr. Hall knows she was a lesbian."

"Well, I don't know what Sarah wants from me," I said. "I'm not Euripides."

"You'll find somebody," said Ethel briskly. "Call me back." And she hung up.

I went over to my bookshelves. My books provided me with most of my Hallmark nominees but this time, as I studied them, my mind kept cracking jokes:

"We nominate Persephone for The Hallmark Hall of Fame *because:* she was the first woman to go to hell and back for her man."

"We nominate Jocasta for The Hallmark Hall of Fame *because:* she was Oedipus' mother and Freud's inspiration."

And then suddenly a book on the top shelf leaned out and waved to me. "Eureka," I said, feeling very Greek, and took the book down and kissed it.

The book was *Imaginary Conversations* by Walter Savage Landor and the conversation in it I loved best was a lyric dialogue between Aesop and a young slave girl named Rhodope (pronounced Rah-do-pay. I think). The dialogue contained no incident or event I could dramatize, but I decided that Aesop and his fables would make a fine nominee and that Sarah would enjoy playing Landor's gentle slave girl. And it was a sunny day on which to walk down through Central Park and on to the Forty-second Street main library to do a little research.

Strolling down through the park, I tried to remember where else I'd read about Rhodope. It seemed to me that somebody else had written about her, but I couldn't remember who it was. Since it was Aesop I was nominating, I stopped trying to place Rhodope and concentrated instead on Aesop's fables. By the time I reached the library I knew just which fables I wanted to use and how I wanted to use them, and I ran up to the third floor and hurried over to the card file marked A and made out library slips for all the books on Aesop.

In an hour I'd read all the library could tell me about Aesop's life because the fact is that nothing at all is known about him for certain. A few books described him as a humpbacked beggar, a few backed Landor's theory that he was a slave and an equal number stated that no such person as Aesop ever lived and that the fables were the work of anonymous writers.

None of the books on Aesop mentioned a slave girl named Rhodope.

Hallmark scripts were supposed to be factual. I had no facts. I found a library phone booth and called Ethel and gave her a digest of my findings.

"Based on Landor's dialogue," I said, "I could write a story about Aesop with a lovely part for Sarah — but I'd have to make it all up."

There was a pause while Ethel studied the problem.

"Here's what you do," she said. "In Sarah's mistress-of-ceremonies introduction, write a line saying that nobody knows anything about Aesop's life. And then add, 'Some say he was a hunchback, some say he never lived — and some say it happened like this. WE say it.' That way, you're not lying but you're not claiming it's factual and you can make up your own story."

"Like a fable!" I cried, carried away.

I hung up, left the booth, hurried past the card catalogue, down the steps and out of the library. And since I'd learned nothing about Aesop and was writing the script for Sarah anyway, I can't tell you why it didn't even cross my mind to stop at the card catalogue marked R and look up Rhodope. All I know is it didn't. I hurried home to reread Landor's dialogue and get to work on the script.

I was positively inspired as I wrote it. I was inspired by Landor's lovely lines, Aesop's fables, the evils of slavery, the glory that was Greece and the fact that I could make up what I needed as I went along. I finished it late one afternoon, proofread it after dinner and then took it over to Ethel Frank's house that evening; she liked working on scripts at home in the evening when it was quiet.

Ethel's mother let me in and told me Ethel was in her bedroom talking on the phone to Albert in Hollywood. I went down the hall and walked into her bedroom just in time to hear Ethel tell Albert, in a tone of high tragedy:

"Helene just quit the show."

"Oh, she couldn't have," I said. "Her teeth aren't paid for."

Ethel waved at me furiously to be quiet. Her face wore the dignified, persecuted look it always wore when she was bawling out Albert. She had an arresting face, with angular cheekbones and wide eyes. Her hair, which was whatever shade Arden's was featuring in any given season, was pale brown with gold streaks that spring.

"I have told you before, Albert, to keep your grubby hands off my writers' scripts," she went on with wounded dignity. "The last time Helene walked off the show I talked her into coming back. This time I don't know whether I can or not."

Albert had a habit of tinkering with dialogue to give it a soap-opera touch. Since I never saw the show, I never knew when he'd got his itchy fingers on one of my scripts until Ethel told me about it afterward, and to avoid getting ulcers over it I refused to read his rewrites. I loved writing for Hallmark, but once a script was finished and out of my hands, the show was over and I went on to the next one. It was Ethel who got the ulcers. She was fiercely protective of her writers.

I sat down on the bed, pushing aside a litter of TV scripts, to wait out the fight, which was the last, and always the longest, of her three daily fights with Albert. The fights had begun a year earlier when the Hallmark show had moved to Hollywood. Albert, of course, had ordered Ethel to move out there with it. Ethel had declined; she didn't like Hollywood.

"I can't produce a show in California with my story editor in New York!" Albert had shouted.

"Fire me," Ethel had advised him sympathetically. But they'd worked together a long time, and since Ethel was the best story editor in the business Albert hadn't been able to bring himself to fire her. So the show was produced in Hollywood with scripts written in New York, necessitating an open telephone line coast-to-coast, on which Ethel conducted her three daily fights. The first took place at 1 P.M. our time and 10 A.M. Albert's time and got him out of bed. (He rehearsed at night and slept late.) The second took place at 4 P.M. our time and 1 P.M. Albert's and took him away from his lunch. And the third began at 10 P.M. our time and disposed of Albert's dinner hour.

"That Albert," Ethel remarked conversationally when she finally hung up. "He's ruining my entire nervous system." She took a tranquilizer — she took one after most evening fights with Albert — and then pointed eagerly to the script in my lap.

"How'd it come out?" she asked.

"Great," I said modestly. Ethel read the script aloud with a stopwatch, and agreed that it was the best little television script in the whole wide world, and we mailed it to Hollywood. A few days later Sarah phoned from Hollywood to tell me how much she liked it, and Albert got on the phone to congratulate me and everybody was happy.

The Hallmark Hall of Fame went on the air at 5 P.M. New York time (2 P.M. Hollywood time) on Sunday afternoons. On the Sunday on which "Aesop and Rhodope" was to be broadcast I was up early and dawdled over breakfast with the Sunday *Times.* As always, I read the theatre section and the front page over breakfast; and with my second cup of coffee I turned to the *Book Review* section. I scanned the review on the front page and then opened the section to pages 2 and 3.

The entire upper half of page 3 was occupied by a review of a book entitled *A House Is Not a Home* by Polly Adler. A headline indicated that Polly Adler was a madam and that her book concerned houses of prostitution. Under the headline was a photograph of the sculptured head of a young girl. Under the photograph, the caption read simply, in neat black italics:

Rhodope, the most famous prostitute in Greece.

Well, there we were. Or rather, since I couldn't wake up Ethel at nine-thirty on a Sunday morning, there I was.

Sitting there spilling coffee all over myself, I remembered *(now I remembered)* where I'd read about Rhodope. I'd come upon her in sketchy accounts of the life of Sappho and in the two or three lines of Sappho's Greek I'd ever been able to read. But in Greek, the spelling of a noun changes with every case, so Rhodope was Rhodope when you talked to her and Rhodopis when you talked about her. Sappho had talked about her. Not flatteringly.

To while away the time till I could break the news to Ethel, I got down a couple of books to see exactly what it was Sappho had said about her. According to the only accounts I had in the house, Rhodope had been a slave until she was thirteen years old, at which age she was set up in business as a prostitute by her owner. Sappho's brother met her, fell in love with her, bought her freedom and took her to live with him. And Rhodope (according to Sappho) took Sappho's brother for every drachma he had and then left him for richer men.

Where Landor got his version of Rhodope as a gentle, innocent maiden I didn't know and still don't.

At ten o'clock it occurred to me that Mr. Joyce C. Hall out in Kansas City, Missouri, subscribed to the Sunday *Times* (he was a TV sponsor and all TV sponsors subscribed to it for the theatre section, which contained TV news, reviews and commentary), and I woke up Ethel.

"What's the matter?" she demanded sleepily on the phone.

"It says on page three of the *Times Book Review* section," I said, "that Rhodope was the most famous prostitute in Greece."

"The most famous what?" said Ethel, wide awake.

"Prostitute," I said. "Her picture's in the paper. They wait two thousand five hundred years and then pick today to put her picture in the paper, surrounded by a review of a book on whorehouses."

Ethel enjoyed crises; they stimulated her.

"Now don't panic," she said briskly. "Let me get the *Book Review* section."

She was gone from the phone for a couple of minutes. Then she came back and said:

"Hang up, let me call Ed in Kansas City, I'll call you back." Ed was the Hallmark account executive. I gathered she had to wake him up, too — it was an hour earlier in Kansas City — because it was some time before she phoned me back.

"Okay," she said. "Ed's driving out to Hall's place, he thinks the *Times* will still be on Hall's front porch and he'll take the *Book Review* section out of it. If they've already taken the *Times* in, he'll ring the bell and ask to borrow the *Book Review* section for his kid."

"What about Albert and Sarah?" I asked.

"They haven't time to read anything on a Sunday, are you kidding?" said Ethel. "They'll be rehearsing clear to air time and then they go out and eat."

"Well, just tell Ed to keep an eye out for the mail," I said. "We're going to be getting letters from college professors —"

"Nobody in this country ever heard of Rhodope but you and Polly Adler," said Ethel. "And even if they have, it's one thing to see the name in print and another thing to hear it pronounced. Who knows how Sarah'll pronounce it? We won't get letters from anybody."

We got two. From two prep-school English teachers who wrote to request copies of the script for their classes and to express the hope that Hallmark would continue to do interesting educational shows of this kind.

By the time Hallmark went off the air, my teeth were capped and paid for and I had two thousand dollars in the bank, making me richer than I'd ever been in my life. But I was also unemployed. And when, one early summer day, notice arrived that

Maudiebird's building was to be renovated and we were all to be evicted, I had no way of knowing what rent I could afford on my next hovel. I had three months to find a place and I was room-hunting in a half-hearted fashion when, one morning, Rosemary phoned. Rosemary was a friend of Ethel's and a former Holly-wood writer.

"Ethel and Albert have a new show," she announced.

"I knew they could do it," I said. "What is it?"

"Well," said Rosemary, "are you sitting down? It's to be called Matinee Theatre and it's going to be an hour dramatic show, produced live and in color from Hollywood, every day."

"You mean every week," I said.

"Every week day," said Rosemary. "Five a week. Albert's the executive producer, Ethel's the associate producer, I'm the chief story editor and you're the chief writer."

"Are you sure, Rosemary?" I asked.

"I'm sure," said Rosemary.

"Hang up," I said. "I have to think."

The chief writer of such a show would be writing a script a month — more, if she could write them faster than that. Pay-checks floated before my eyes in heady profusion. The time had come which I'd begun to believe would never come: I was finally through with garrets. I was going to get myself a home.

One week later I signed a three-year lease on an apartment in a brand-new luxury building. It had a large living room, a small alcove big enough for bookshelves, a desk and my typewriter, a flossy new kitchen and a shiny new tile bath. I blew my entire savings on furniture and drapes and wall-to-wall carpet, and on a day in October I moved in. A big, good-natured guy named Her-bie arrived early in the morning to lay the carpet, and when he finished that afternoon, he insisted on uncrating the new furniture for me and distributing it around at my direction. And as long as I live I will never forget the moment when he shoved the last end table and lamp into place, and I stood in the middle of my own home and looked around and said:

"It's beautiful."

And I didn't even know I was crying till Herbie said:

"Well, it's nothin' to bawl about, honey!"

Two days later, Rosemary moved into a flat on the floor above mine, and you have no idea what having her overhead meant to me in the three wild and woolly years of Matinee Theatre. All the other Matinee writers had to run down to Radio City to Ethel's office all the time. I never had to leave the house. Rosemary would come home at six, bringing me a book or play to adapt. I'd write the first draft and when it was finished leave it in her mailbox. She'd read it the next day, leave the office an hour early and come to my apartment for cocktails and a story conference. I'd write the revisions and then run up the back stairs to her apartment with the final version, and she'd take it to the office the next morning and bring home a new assignment for me that evening.

I say "that evening" because nobody connected with the show ever got a day off. Matinee Theatre was the most frenzied operation in the history of television.

Out in Hollywood, under Albert McCleery, were two assistant producers, ten directors, two story editors and twenty writers. In New York, under Ethel, were three readers, two story editors and fifty to sixty writers. There were five plays in rehearsal in Hollywood at all times. On a given Sunday, Monday's show would be in its sixth and last day of rehearsal, Tuesday's in its fifth day, Wednesday's in its fourth — and so on, with Albert overseeing (presumably by bicycle) all five. In New York, all Ethel Frank had to do was find twenty properties a month, clear the literary rights, assign the scripts, read and approve the final edited versions and mail them to Hollywood at a rate which ensured a backlog of a month's scripts.

With so many scripts to assign, Ethel was frequently forced to gamble on new and untried writers, and every few months one of them turned in an unusable script. Since there was no money in the budget for a new script, the crisis might have been acute. Thanks to me — Miss Big-Mouth — Matinee Theatre found a simple solution to the problem.

The first day an unproducible script was turned in, Rosemary read it and left it on Ethel's desk with a note:

"Ethel: This is a dog. What do we do now?"

It happened that on that day I finished a script just before lunch. I took advantage of the rare, free afternoon to stroll down through the park and on to Rockefeller Center to pay a social call on my friends in the Matinee Theatre office. I wandered into Ethel's private office and found her sunk in gloom. She showed me Rosemary's note and then invited me to read the first page of the "dog." The script was not just unproducible, it was illiterate.

"What do you do when this happens?" I asked.

"What can I do?" Ethel demanded. "We've got a hundred dollars left in the budget! I can't get a script written on that!"

Ethel was my friend, wasn't she? Thanks to her, I was making piles of money and living in a breathtaking one-and-a-half-room palace, wasn't I?

"I'll do it over for you, Ethel," I said.

"We could only pay you a hundred bucks for it!" cried Ethel. (An hour script paid a thousand.)

"That's all right, Ethel," I said.

"You'd have to write a whole new script!" cried Ethel.

"That's all right, Ethel," I said.

"We need it in a week!" cried Ethel. (An hour script normally took four weeks or five.)

"That's all right, Ethel," I said.

I hurried home with the crisis assignment, I slaved for seven days and seven evenings and managed to turn in the script on time. Ethel and Rosemary read it and liked it and showered me with praise and gratitude and admiration, and what the two of them did to me from then on I have trouble believing, even now. As Rosemary had the nerve to reconstruct one of their typical crisis conversations for me, it went like this:

I'd be hard at work trying to reduce *Pride and Prejudice* to eight characters and fifty minutes, while down at the Matinee office Rosemary was hurrying into Ethel's office with an illiterate script and the dread pronouncement: "It's a dog!"

"It can't be!" Ethel would snarl. "Albert's hired a star for it! It goes into rehearsal next Monday!"

"Well, you're going to have to get a new script written in three days, then!" Rosemary would say. And she and Ethel would eye each other.

"How," Ethel would inquire delicately, "is she feeling?"

"I could ask her," Rosemary would offer nervously.

"I'll do it," Ethel would say. "She can hold up on *Pride and Prejudice* till the weekend and still finish on time; she's fast."

A minute later my phone would ring and Ethel would ask brightly:

"How do you feel, hon? Do you feel strong?"

Occasionally it was Rosemary who phoned and, in a voice dripping with catastrophe, said:

"Dear, we're in a *terrible* jam, I *know* how tired you are, but —"

I resurrected so many dead dogs for Matinee that after a while, when the phone rang, a sixth sense told me Ethel or Rosemary was at the other end with another dog, and I'd pick up the phone and say briskly:

"City Pound."

I couldn't sign my name to those scripts, of course. The only person who could legally rewrite unusable scripts without being paid for it was the story editor. So each time, I was put on the show's payroll as a story editor. But since story editors were not entitled to screen credit for the rewriting they did, it was necessary for me to have a pseudonym. If you ever run across a television script by Herman Knight, I wrote it. Herman wasn't great but he was dirt-cheap and fast as the wind.

Herman and I were both worn out by the beginning of Matinee's third year. I was working on the adaptation of a disorganized Chinese fantasy called *The Carefree Tree*, when the phone rang and a secretary said: "Ethel Frank calling."

"Hon," said Ethel. "Drop *The Carefree Tree*, you can go back to it later. Come on down, I have a special assignment for you."

"No," I said.

"It's not a dog, it's a big assignment!" said Ethel, and added solemnly: "We have a new sponsor. You're going to do their first show."

This so thoroughly baffled me I left *The Carefree Tree* in the typewriter and went down to the Matinee office out of sheer curiosity.

The cost of producing Matinee five days a week, live and in color, meant that the show was shared by four or five sponsors. This multiple sponsorship kept the show, and the writers, beyond the reach of corporation or ad agency interference, since no sponsor could hope to control a show of which he owned only one fifth. Plus which, sponsors were constantly signing on and dropping off the Matinee roster the way you'd hop on or off a bus. I couldn't imagine any sponsor whose arrival Ethel would announce with such solemnity.

She and Rosemary were in a huddle over a list of names when I walked in.

Ethel looked up.

"We're going to produce a series of special plays," she said, "for the United Lutheran Church in America."

It shook me. It shook all three of us.

"You're going to write the first script," said Ethel. "We're buying that Ozark play you liked, if the Lutherans okay it."

"Ethel," I said, "do you think I'm the ideal writer for the United Lutheran Church?"

Ethel looked pious.

"The Lutherans," she intoned, "are remarkable men. They told me they do not have the slightest interest in the religious denomination of the writer."

"That may very well be," I said, "but I doubt if they had Reform Judaism in mind."

Rosemary laughed.

"All I need on this show is to run around trying to find six Lutheran writers," said Ethel bitterly.

"Well, we ought to find them a Lutheran story editor, dear!" said Rosemary. Rosemary had a Catholic father and a Methodist mother, the other story editor was Jewish, and neither of them had time to take on additional scripts.

It was several days later that Ethel phoned to say she'd found a story editor for the Lutherans and I went down to the office and met Katherine, a gentle, blonde Episcopalian. (Said Ethel morosely: "In this town they're lucky I found them a Protestant.")

In a simple black dress with a white collar and a retiring violet lipstick, Katherine was pronounced very holy-looking, and she trotted off to meet the Lutherans with the Ozark play under her arm. The play was the story of a fifteen-year-old girl in the backwoods of Arkansas, all of whose yearnings were focused on a red dress in a mail-order catalogue. Neglected by ignorant parents and ignored by a preoccupied schoolteacher, the girl allowed a boy to make love to her in return for money to buy the red dress; she became pregnant and was driven to a fatal, self-inflicted abortion. I had read the play a few years earlier for Monograph and had recommended it to Ethel as one we might somehow sanitize for television.

The Lutherans liked the play, and they didn't want it sanitized. They wanted plays that dealt with the problems confronting all mid-twentieth-century churches, and the teenager's tragedy was grimly familiar to them. They approved the script and directed that it be produced as their Easter show.

Katherine and I worked hard on the script, and when it was finished copies were sent to the six Lutherans in charge of the project. All six read the script and then invited Katherine and me to a dinner conference to discuss revisions. They were charming hosts and it wasn't till coffee was served that the six copies of the script were passed to Katherine and me, each with notes in the margins suggesting revisions. All the revisions were minor. But one particular margin note appeared prominently on every script: "WHERE EASTER?" My heritage had caught up with me; I'd gone and left Easter out of the Easter script.

We assured the Lutherans that Easter would be prominently featured in the final version, the conference ended and I went home to do the revisions. A week later, the final revised script was approved by the Lutherans and airmailed to Albert in Hollywood. It went into rehearsal on a Thursday.

On Friday, the NBC censorship office telephoned Albert and ordered him to cancel the show. NBC censorship was sent a copy of every Matinee script as a matter of form, and the only one it ever ordered off the air as too immoral for the television industry was the first script sponsored by the Lutheran Church.

Ethel, Rosemary and Katherine sat in the East Coast Matinee office that afternoon in a kind of paralysis, wondering how to tell the Lutherans they were too sinful for television. But out in Hollywood, Albert McCleery was phoning NBC, beginning with the censorship office and working his way straight up to the top-level executives, repeating the same message to each:

"You go ahead and cancel this show," he was shouting, "and I'll see to it that every newspaper from New York to California carries the story of how NBC censored the Lutheran Church off the air!"

Late that afternoon, NBC backed down and rehearsals of the play were allowed to proceed.

My last unsettling experience unsettled me clear out of the Annex.

Not long after Matinee Theatre went off the air, I won a fellowship from CBS. I was given five thousand dollars on which to work for a year on TV dramatizations of American history. Sitting in the bathtub, the day after I won this contest, I made a momentous decision: henceforth I would stop looking down on television. I would stop writing bad plays and commit myself unreservedly to television scripts. I even toyed with the possibility of buying a TV set.

Fired by this decision, I flung myself into the fellowship year. I researched for months in libraries, I wrote a ninety-minute script, rewrote it under the supervision of one of the Playhouse 90 producers and then plunged into a series of outlines for more ninety-minute scripts to come.

And all this time, behind my back, television, which had waited to do it till I'd made my great bathtub decision, now went completely to pot. First, the quiz-show scandals broke. Then the CBS executives in charge of the fellowship project were forced out of CBS. Then Playhouse 90 went off the air. Then every other dramatic show went off the air, to be replaced by Gunsmoke, Perry Mason, and fifty imitations of each. Most devastating of all, I woke up at the end of my fellowship year to discover that the entire television industry had packed up and moved to Hollywood where it was now permanently resettled.

I was unwilling (to put it mildly) to follow Gunsmoke and Perry Mason to Hollywood; westerns bored me and nothing could induce me to revert to shabby TV whodunits. No need to worry, I told myself. Ethel and Albert were bound to get a new show, produced in Hollywood and written in New York.

And sure enough, one day in the fall of 1960, Ethel phoned with the long-awaited words:

"Albert and I have a new show."

"Hallelujah," I said. "What is it?"

"I just want you to realize," said Ethel, "that we're almost the only show that's still written on the East Coast. And East or West, dear, if you want to work in television you're going to have to write for this kind of show. It's all they're doing now."

"Ethel," I said, "what's the show?"

"The Adventures of Ellery Queen," she said.

Please Use Nearest Exit

Dec. 6? 7? '60

Now listen, Maxine —

As soon as we hung up the other night I phoned those girls you sublet to and told them about your green deck chair and your good stew pot and they are mailing the stew pot to Hollywood today by Parcel Post but they said to tell you you do not HAVE a green deck chair. They looked in the closet where you said it probably was, and the cellar storeroom where you said it would be if it wasn't in the closet, and it isn't in either place and it also isn't anywhere else, you probably hocked it.

This is not a real letter because (a) you already owe me two letters and (b) I'm late for the Unemployment Insurance office.

WRITE ME.

love

h.

Dear Heart —

I know I said on my Christmas card I'd write soon and here it is March but I've been busy making my movie debut.

First, did you know when you see "(MOS)" in a shooting script it means MidOut Sound? Comes from way back in the days of the early talkies when some German was directing a movie and at one point he shouted: "Ve do zis next take midout sound!" So of course they've been writing (MOS) in shooting scripts ever since.

Now about my movie debut. I bumped into Joe Anthony on the street and he told me he was directing *Career* and he'd try and get me a bit in it. The next day I got a call from Paramount and would I come in and meet Hal Wallis, producer of *Career*? I went in and met him — I was very charming and commented on the chic of his office, his sweater, his tan and anything else I could see — and he said I could report to the casting director of *Career* the next day, there was a part in it for me.

So the casting director gave me a script and told me which scene to study. There were two characters in the scene — CHIC WOMAN IN HER MID-THIRTIES and MIDDLE-AGED TV DIRECTOR, both parts maybe five lines long. I started reading the CHIC WOMAN IN HER MID-THIRTIES and he said: "No, you're the TV director."

Well, lemme tell you it was a blow to the ego, but I started reading the TV director till I got to a line in the business where it said the chic woman "hands HIM a book."

So that night I called my agent and said: "Listen, there's been a mistake; they've got me playing a man. And if it costs Paramount Pictures half a million when they find out the mistake and have to retake the whole scene, somebody's gonna get a poker up. So you better check with Paramount."

The next day when they got ready to shoot the scene I met *both* the chic woman who'd been hired to play the chic woman *and* the middle-aged gent who'd been hired to play the TV director. It seems Mr. Wallis can't stand to see people out of work so he keeps hiring three or four people for the same bit part, regardless of sex. So they made the TV director a woman and let me play that, and they gave the nice middle-aged gentleman two lines to say someplace else, and that's how Muzzy got into the movies, kiddies.

I'm homesick. Spring has come to California and it puts me in mind of little goodies like Radio City and Bloomingdale's but let's face it, I'm working out here. I've done five TV shows in the last two months.

And that's the story of my life and *please* write and tell me about yours, your last letter around Christmas was very disquieting. You must have found gainful employment by now, please God?

love

m.

305 E. 72nd St. STILL!
(even though the rent just
went up again)

Doll!

I'm getting up a party of hundreds to go see *Career* and cheer and stomp when you come on.

I have mildly earthshaking news of my own which I'm sitting

here celebrating with a rare and beautiful martini — You should see me, running around this opulent, wall-to-wall palace in slacks with patches in the seat and sweaters with holes in the elbow, putting quarters in a piggy-bank till they mount up to a bottle of gin. Hysterical.

Anyhow, here I was with my unemployment insurance running out and the bells ringing in a New Year and suddenly for the first time I faced the fact that I was NOT between assignments, I was NOT temporarily out of work, I was permanently out of a profession. And I thought: "What are you DOING, sitting here waiting for television to move back East and turn respectable or somebody to buy one of your old plays? Television is not coming back East and nobody's going to buy your plays, they're all terrible. If you want to eat for the rest of your life you'd better try writing something else."

So I got down the old play about *Oklahoma!* and decided if I deleted the junky plot and just told the straight facts it might make a magazine article. Slaved over it for three weeks and sent it to *Harper's* and damned if *Harper's* didn't buy it. Sent me a letter of acceptance and $200. Before-taxes-and-agent's-commission but think of the presTIGE, *Harper's* kept telling me.

Carried away by this success, I got down the old play about Stokowski and turned it into what I hoped was a *New Yorker* story and sent it off to *The New Yorker* and a week later one of their editors phoned to say he liked it and *The New Yorker* was buying it.

Well, I like to fall down dead with joy. Every day for the next week I hurried down for the mail, looking for the check and the letter-of-acceptance or whatever they called their contract. It didn't come. So I wrote to the gent who'd phoned, saying Would he please send me a contract; and I added: "You didn't say on the phone how much *The New Yorker* is paying me. Is it a secret?"

It was a secret. He didn't answer my letter. And he didn't send a contract.

Two weeks later the galleys arrived — which is how I knew they'd "bought" the story. A week after that, the story appeared in print. On the day the issue of *The New Yorker* with my story in it turned up on the newsstands, a check came in the mail from *The New Yorker* for $400.

I tore up the street to the bank with it, and standing at the teller's window I turned the check over, to endorse it.

On the back of the check, rubber-stamped and bleeding off the edge of the paper, was the contract.

When I endorsed the check, I automatically signed the contract — which then went back to *The New Yorker* as a canceled check.

So cancel your *New Yorker* subscription and rush RIGHT out and subscribe to the *Reader's Digest*. They don't believe in contracts either — but they picked up the *Harper's* story for reprint and paid me more for it than *Harper's* and *The New Yorker* put together. The check just came this morning — along with a letter from an editor at Harper & Row, Book Publishers, saying she liked the *Oklahoma!* story in *Harper's* and Do I have a book in mind? No, I do not have a book in mind but the letter made my day, who else ever asked me such a high-brow question?

I think my potroast is burning.

love

h.

MISS MAXINE STUART
1105 MERILLON AVENUE
LOS ANGELES CALIFORNIA

HARPERS WANTS ME TO WRITE MY AUTOBIOGRAPHY HOW TO GET NOWHERE IN THE THEATRE YOU'RE COSTARRING SEND REMINIS-CENCES IT TURNS OUT I SPENT ALL THOSE YEARS TRYING TO WRITE PLAYS JUST SO I COULD WRITE A BOOK ABOUT IT AFTERWARDS IS THAT THE LIVING END LOVE

HELENE

MISS HELENE HANFF
305 EAST 72ND STREET
NEW YORK CITY

DARLING AM HYSTERICAL WITH EXCITEMENT ITS NOT THE LIVING
END ITS FLANAGANS LAW LOVE AND CHEERS

MAXINE

Helene Hanff's autobiographical *Underfoot in Show Business* was her first book and was written soon after she completed the exhausting adventures related therein.

Her books since then have included *84, Charing Cross Road, The Duchess of Bloomsbury Street,* and *Apple of My Eye.* All three books are still in print in hardcover and/or paperback both in England and in the United States.